"Each of us has ⊢
and our future ren

Friendly FIRE!

CONFLICT RESOLUTION

Uzziah B. Cooper Sr.

Editor's note: Scripture references are found in the back of the book, at the beginning of the appendices. Unless otherwise indicated, all Scripture quotations are from King James Version of the Holy Bible. Scripture quotations marked (RSV) are from the American Standard Edition of the Revised Version of the Holy Bible. Scripture quotations marked (NASB) are from the New American Standard Bible, 1960, 1962, 1963, 1968, 1971, 1972, 1973, 1975, 1977, 1978 by The Lockman Foundation. Scripture quotations marked (ASV) are from the American Standard Edition of the Revised Version of the Holy Bible. Scripture quotations marked (NIV) are from The Holy bible, New International Version, 1973, 1978, 1984 by the International Bible Society. Used by Permission of Zondervan. Scripture quotations marked (WEY) are from Weymouth New Testament. Scripture quotations marked (BBE) are from Bible in Basic English. Scripture quotations marked (ERV) are from English Revised Version. Scripture quotations marked (WEB) are from World English Bible. All rights reserved. Scripture quotations marked (AB) are from the Amplified Bible. Unless specified, word-study entries are taken from The Complete Word Study Dictionary, New Testament, World Bible Publishers, Inc.

Purchase Friendly Fire
@
http://friendlyfire.org

Dr. Uzziah B. Cooper Sr.

ISBN: 978-1-59684-877-1

Copyright © 2015

By

Uzziah B. Cooper, Sr.
All Rights Reserved

Dedication

To my parents, Eulon Kendal Cooper Sr. and Alice Louise Taylor-Cooper, who departed from their labors for their Heavenly rewards.

Heartfelt gratitude to Dad and Mom! Your untiring and unselfish love and care for your family will never go unnoticed and your many sacrifices for our wellbeing will forever be cherished. God is answering your many prayers for each of your children to become successful through Christ. Rest in peace!

To all who have helped to equip me to become both a Christian leader and a vocational professional; thank you!

Acknowledgment

I am thankful for the privilege to formulate my thoughts and reflect some of them on paper. Without the illumination of Fiery Anointing, I could not have chronically represented these ideas for my reading audience. To this, I acknowledge the mercies of God; the ultimate source of my life. Thank you for your truth, and thank you for Your Anointing to lead others.

This book is a snippet of my life learning and experiences. I consider it to be a collection of the contributions of many mentors, teachers, supporters, advisors, friends, and family. I humbly acknowledge that I am the sum total of what I have learned, as well as the contributions made by so many other people to my life.

Thanks to Mel for your scrutiny of this manuscript, as an independent reader.

Thanks to my immediate family for your many contributions.

CONTENTS

Section	Page
Warming-Up!	13
Fiery Reactions	17
It Only Takes a Spark	24
Fiery Trials	36
Dousing the FirE.	50
Take Out the Log	66
Be On One Accord	74
Glorify God from the Fire.	87
Conclusion	100
About the Author	128
Summary	136

WARMING-UP!

Why are people so often in rage? *(Psalm 2:1 ASV)*. Anger breaths rage and rage will produce conflicts.

Conflict resolution is a bumper-crop and the time is 'NOW' for Christendom to lead in resolving them. Resolving conflicts assures harmonious relationships, peaceable communities and a better world. At best, human faults can only be resolved through perpetual reconciliation with and forgiveness of each other. Conflicts will continue to rage, unless harmony is regarded as a key ingredient for lasting relationships. In spite of quarrelsome situations, visible healthy indicators are necessary signs of progress with the rebuilding of faltering relationship. It is a fact that the Biblical principal of "being on one accord" is foundational in showing that conflicts are being effectively managed.

Numerous methods and remedies have been formulated by the best of scholars throughout the centuries, to safeguard against threatening of conflicts upon relationships. Many masterful renditions are available for all to follow, so that they could avoid conflicts. Contrary-wise, many questions continue: Why is brokenness so prevalent among relationships? What is causing the proliferation of family feud and break-downs? How can grievances be mitigated before they are escalated into cruel bloodshed? Why are vibrant religious and financially sound organizations splitting-up?

Conflicts are often set ablaze when a flaming tongue burns into the integrity of others, leaving behind painful scars and embarrassment. Conflicts occur because the lives of individuals are complex; nonetheless, conflicts must be disallowed from spreading like wildfire. Effective management of crises is one way whereby crises can be controlled, but relying on the supernatural in the midst of crises is paramount. Rage, anger, crises and conflicts are common to all, but *"God will provide a way out so that* (All) *can stand up under it" (1 Corinthians 10:13 NIV).*

Conflicts are joy-killers! They seek out and entrap the liberties of soon to be victims, leaving them gasping for another gulp of harmonious-oxygen. Like wildfire, these disruptions will eventually strangle any living being or any living thing, thus rendering them comatose. Conflicts do not know boundaries, they are hardly controlled, nor do they have regard for neither humankind nor anything which is in their space. Although conflicts emit energies that are disruptive, setting ablaze clashes and crises, there is hope. The fiery darts of the enemy can be quenched, when there is consideration for the soon to be victim. Speak life instead of insults, cursing, or accusations and the unnecessary relational commotions will be minimized.

Conflicts can be conditions which are destructive to relationships of every type. The infernos of conflicts are scorching hot, melting the fasteners which hold sound reasoning together. Conflicts are debilitating; they do not know holistic ethics, shame, boundaries, nationalities, cultures, religions, race, creed or color. Conflicts become their own governance to themselves, without consideration for peaceable resolves.

Conflicts are cancerous, never slowing their efforts until personalities become malignant, care for each other is replaced with jealousy and relationships become marred. When allowed, unresolved relational conflicts eradicate entire generations, but there is a way of escape from this deadly relational menace.

To those who serve in supporting roles, conflicts will be minimized when there is a "buy in" into the vision of leadership. Leaders can discourage conflicts by embracing those who desire to build with their vision. *"Love* (respect) *your neighbor as yourself" (Leviticus 19:18, Mark 12:31).* Leaders and laity/subordinates within their common faith groups must maintain a common bond. Holding up the shield of faith, in concert, must be continuous in all forms, in order to stem the fiery arrows of conflicts.

"It should not be surprising to know, that most world religions affirm a basic principle of fair play. Although there will be no discussion as to what these religions state as the 'golden rule', there is no surprise that the following quotes below make similar claim, at least on the surface, to the quote above from Mark and Leviticus"[1]. {"Not one of you is a believer until he loves for his brother what he loves for himself" *Islam.* Forty Hadith of an-

Nawawi 13; "A man should wander about treating all creatures as he himself would be treated" *Jainism*. Sutrakritanga 1.11.33; "Try your best to treat others as you would wish to be treated yourself, and you will find that this is the shortest way to benevolence" *Confucianism*. Mencius VII.A.4; "One should not behave towards others in a way which is disagreeable to oneself. This is the essence of morality. All other activities are due to selfish desire" *Hinduism*. Mahabharata, Anusasana Parva 113.8}.[2]

All are charged with the responsibility of building harmonious relationships, so that they can enjoy the comfort of friendly fire. Religious organizations are equally mandated to strangle conflicts and remain both current and effective in a simmering world. Harmonious relationships will be realized when family persons think, speak, experience and believe that which constitutes them as "family".

When overtaken by conflicts, glorify God while yet in the fiery crucible. Forgive those who are heating the flames and allow Fiery Anointing to burn away ills of discords and contentions. When given a chance, there will be a time of refreshing. If an end is not made of warring, war will put an end to the fighters.

-1-

FIERY REACTIONS

Fire is a natural force central to God's order, and is most important to civilization. It can be classified as nature's most terrifying force, possessing unlimited destructive powers. Fire destroys homes, religious houses, civic centers and commercial establishments, along with all contents and occupancies, within a short period of time. Fire can reduce an entire forest to a pile of ash and charred wood within a short period of time.

Fire kills more people every year than any other force of nature. There are few things which have done as much harms to humanity as fire, yet fewer things which have done as much good for the benefit of human survival. Fire is particularly necessary for the wellbeing of humankind. It provides the original form of portable light and heat for comfort, affords the opportunities to cook meals and forges metal tools, used to form pottery and hardens bricks, and is necessary to drive power engines. It is certainly one of the most important forces in human history. But what exactly is fire?

The ancient Greeks considered fire to be one of the major elements in the universe, alongside heaven, water, earth and air. This grouping makes intuitive sense, since fire, earth, water and are considered as wonders of the world. Fire can be seen, smelt and move from place to place, but fire is really something completely different than heaven, water, earth and air. Earth, water and air are all forms of matter. They are made up of millions and millions of atoms collected together. Fire is not matter at all. It is a visible, tangible side effect of 'matter' changing form, while at the same time, a chemical reaction.

Although incredible and devastating to nature, yet our God delivers both by and from fire. Ancient Israel was delivered out of the iron-smelting furnace, out of Egypt *(Deuteronomy 4:20)*. Because Shadrach, Meshach, and Abednego refused to fall down and worship the golden image which King Nebuchadnezzar erected as a god, the king in his rage and fury commanded that the three young men be bound and cast into a fiery furnace. To the king's surprise, his fury could not subject his would-be victims to his crucible of rage. God, who is all powerful, delivered the three Hebrew young men out of the fire. He is all omnipotent!

As a young teenager, I witnessed God's delivering power of my family from fire. One dark night, my father decided that he would fuel his pick-up truck, for a pre-dawn journey to Rolleville from Forbes Hill, Exuma, Bahamas. Economic times were difficult and few families lived on the island. Among other things, modern technology for the fueling of motor vehicles was predominantly non-existent on the island. Dad imported gasoline from Nassau in units of fifty-five gallons drums, for the fueling and operating of his pickup truck. His process for refueling was to cipher gasoline from the drum into a gasoline jug and then reverse the process from the jug to the pickup fuel tank.

One pitch-dark night, dad proceeded to fuel his pickup. Neither my Dad nor any of my siblings present at the drum were able to determine the level of the gasoline in the jug. Being conscious of the gasoline overflowing onto the ground, Dad scratched a match to provide light, but got an inferno instead. The gasoline fumes ignited and consumed the jug. Dad's reactions were immediate, picking up the blazing jug, placed it on his shoulder and ran away from the drum. He pitched the blazing jug into a sandy area on the other side of the main street. Dad's quick response spared our lives from the real possibility of a fiery disaster. Years later, I connected this experience to one of God's fiery promise: *"when thou walkest through the fire, thou shalt not be burned" (Isaiah 43:2).*

Oftentimes, God has showed-up in forms of fire, to which there were always reactions. The LORD appeared to Moses in a blazing fire from the midst of *a bush*. As Moses looked on the blaze, the bush was burning, but the bush was not consumed. In his reaction to the burning bush, Moses thought it strange that the bush was not burning *(Exodus 3:3)*. Another reaction by Moses was when he hid his face from God, as God commanded him not to go any closer to the fire. God also commanded Moses, in this vision, to lead His people out of the fires of conflicts, just as He expects today's leaders to do.

A chemical reaction between oxygen in the atmosphere and matter (fuel, wood, paper, etc) produces fire. No, matter does not spontaneously catch on fire just because they are surrounded by oxygen. A combustible reaction happens when matter is heated to its ignitable temperature. Like fire, negative reactions to adverse social behaviors precipitate social tensions, conflicts and fierce exchange of words. These kinds of tensions oftentimes develop into aggravation, before smoldering into conflict, grudges and violence. Aggravation, a compound condition like smoke, is fed by oxygen from 'the prince of the air'.

Almost always, when humankind is *"Abid(ing) in the vine …" (John 15:4)* and practicing good hermeneutics of Scripture, they resist the urge of reacting negatively to 'the prince of the power of the air'. Wholesome relationships are nurtured between two or more persons through mutually shared respect. As they desire comrade, quality time together will bind those in common relationships together. Showing the same care for each other, *(1 Corinthians 15:25),* is an indicator that this Scripture text are understood and practices hermeneutically.

Moment by moment, the world's population, approximately seven billion people, experience the heat from conflict crucibles. As medical sciences continue to advance, this population will swell proportionally and societal ills will continue to burn through these advancements. Social ills identified by Scripture are sexual immorality, impurity and debauchery; idolatry and witchcraft; hatred, discord, jealousy, fits of rage, selfish ambition, dissensions, factions and envy; drunkenness, orgies, and the like *(Galatians*

5:19-21 NIV). While these ills continue their onslaught of social conflicts, all must continue to stand against them, so that the victory over conflicts can be won. *"Every child of God defeats this evil world through faith" (1 John 5:4 NLT).*

Each social ill has unique attractions and trappings, which can fuel conflict's fiery infernos in one form or another. These fueling are spiritual warfare and human strength should not be the acceptable safeguard against them, for those who desire to escape them. Suffocating these agents will not be accomplished through natural strength, but by employing those special tools, skills and calling which are by the Power of God. I submit, only by this power can all become quickened to overcome the evil of conflicts.

While individuals contribute to conflict resolution methods, group efforts to eradicate conflicts are more effective most times. An example is for leader and laity of the same faith community to maintain a united effort, as they work together to a preferred future. Ideology without the power of Fiery Anointing will vanish away. Fiery Anointing is the sustaining power for the bringing together of leader and laity, for the perfecting of common goals. Common ideology among group members can give birth to singleness of purpose, both mentally and through exploits by the group *(1 Corinthians 1:10 NIV)*.

Conflict is that which comes into collision or disagreement with harmony. Be it contradiction or opposition, conflict is an emotional clash between ideas, feeling, thoughts or personalities. These emotional or psychological breakdowns are often manifested through the articulation of this behavior through words, rage, physical fights, battles, or emotional struggles. Sustained conflicts can be expressed through hatred, grudges, or intentional enactments of prejudice, injustice or inequity. Psychiatrists define conflict as "mental struggles arising from opposing demands or impulses, which are very common in "left-brain / right-brain clashes".

Here, is a simplistic exercise which demonstrates conflicts between the right and left hemispheres of the brain. Although this exercise seems trivial, it is more defining than one would like to think. When looking at a word chart consisting of multi-colored words, different responses are triggers. The right brain is compelled to trigger a pronunciation of the word, but the left brain simultaneously triggers a pronunciation of the color of the same word. This theory of the structure and functions of the mind suggests that the two different sides of the brain control two different modes of thinking.

The following table illustrates basic differences between left-brain and right-brain behavior. Most individuals have a distinct preference for one of these two styles of thinking. Some, however, are more whole-brain and adept equally to both modes of thinking. General scholarships tend to favor left-brain modes of thinking, while downplaying right-brain modes. Left-brain scholastic subjects focus on logical thinking, analysis, and accuracy. Right-brained subjects, on the other hand, focus on aesthetics, feeling and creativity.

Left Brain	**Right Brain**
Logical, sequential	Random
Rational	Intuitive
Analytical	Holistic Synthesizing
Objective	Subjective
Looks at parts	Looks at whole

As it is possible to curve right/left brain behavior to a more holistic way of thinking, humankind can learn how to react positively to conflicts. Remember, negative responses worsen conditions.

"When we are slandered, we answer kindly. Up to this moment we have become the scum of the earth, the refuse of the world" (1 Corinthians 4:13 NIV).

-2-

IT ONLY TAKES A SPARK

Among the greatest celebrations in Israel of ancient times was the "Feast of Tabernacles". One of the most significant features of the observance of this feast occurred at night. At the close of the work day, all roads led to the ceremonial worship which took place at the "Court of Women" of the temple at Jerusalem. In adherence to the guidelines and customs of the feast, four great candlesticks were lit by a spark from a torch and the priests danced until morning, holding the flaming candlestick in their hands. These flames created a symbol of the "great light" which the prophet of old saw through the telescope of time: *"the people that walked in darkness have seen a great light:" (Isaiah 9:2).*

Amidst the customs of the feast of the tabernacle, there could not have been a more opportune time for the Incarnate One to have been announced as the "Light". Before then, custom made it easy for religious leaders to combine the lights of the candlestick and the light of the torch as the prophetic "light". Equally so, were conflict and doubt regarding the purpose and the legitimacy of this light. While some saw this as the true light, others saw it as a light of lesser significant. Yet others saw it as a simple light with a single purpose of masking the darkness of the night.

Imagine the pinnacle of the candle flame seen by those present in the 'Court of Women'. To some, it could have appeared as the nib of a feathered-pen ready to be dipped into a flask of ink, as the Master-Penman recorded His redemptive plan, (the moment of truth). When The Master took hold of this proverbial pen, He architected His plan for Jesus to come to mother earth to rescue fallen humankind from spiritual darkness.

In the beginning God exposed utter darkness when He decreed, *"let there be light" (Genesis 1:3)*. All knowledge and trademark for the formula of converting total darkness to light was and remains His alone. As he created yet another world-order, light stepped forth never again to be contained. His omniscience, to command change keeps His patent trademarked, as Fiery Anointing holds civilization in its orbit. *"But when the fullness of the time was come, God sent forth his Son,.... To redeem them that were under the law" (Galatians 4:4-5)*.

Faith and confidence in the symbolic light continued as a measure of the spirituality of people. Many believed that the light of the torch and candlestick was that which Isaiah prophesied of. Yet, others questioned their lack of understanding that the prophetic light must have been greater than the light from the candle and the torch, by the hands of mortal men. Although they did not fully realize the Divine impact of the prophetic *light*, Jesus remains *"the light of the world" (John 8:12)*.

Those who thought that the combined light of the torches and candle was the real deal soon realized the conflicts which dualism brought. As doubts about the authenticity of the symbolic light entered the minds of many, leaders began to see rapid attrition of their influences upon their followings. Undoubtedly, many questions were asked, as some wanted to know if the religious leadership of that day were standing in contempt. Yet in the midst of these dilemmas, a bombshell was dropped by He who came to fulfill the prophetic light. "Jesus' declaration, "*I am the light of the world,*" not only stunned the religious sects of His day, but sets Christendom at odds with the religious muscles of time to come"[3]. There is hardly a greater conflict to the natural mind than faith in He who came to be the "light of the world".

"The term 'dualism' has a variety of usages in the history of thought. In general, the idea is that, for some particular domain, there are two fundamental kinds or categories of things or principles. In theology, for example a 'dualist' is someone who believes that good and evil - or God and the Devil - are independent and more or less equal forces in the world. Dualism is a contrast to monism, which is the theory that there is only one fundamental kind, category of thing or principle; and, rather less commonly, with pluralism, which is the view that there are many kinds or categories"[4].

There is hardly a time when a prototype of an object would superimpose its reflection upon the real object. Rightly so, it is possible not to know the difference between the real and the reflection of the same. When reasoning fail to separate the real from its shadow, a referral to He who created the object which is producing the shadow becomes necessary. *"The sun is the light to rule the day and the moon and the stars to rule the night" (Psalm 136:8-9).* He who made the sun, moon and stars owns the heavens from which they hang and the patent to the shadows which they cast off.

Religious leaders were amazed by Jesus' miracles but devastated when He announced himself as *the light of the world*. This *light* is the test of truth and the balance of that which is being weighed. He is the witness for all standards and the conscience for that which is not being presented for scrutiny. This *light* exposes anger & contentions and delivers humankind from the clutches of conflicts. Because of this *light*, concerns and care for others are constantly released into the atmosphere with humility.

This is the light which guides all through life's journeys. Equally so, when dark secrets of the inner-being show up, surprising even those who incubated these thoughts, this *light* reveals the intents of their hearts. Not only does this *light* reminds humankind of God's authority over the wiles of the enemy, but also of His assurance to those who are desirous of knowing true harmony; the heart is *"the spring of life" (Proverbs 4:23 NASB).*

In one of Jesus' most heart-wrenching homilies, "*The Sermon on the Mount*", He likens those of the Faith-Community to *light*. It is then reasonable to conclude that He gives these persons power of attorney through His declaration: *"Ye are the light of the world" (Matthew 5:14).* Therefore, it is neither conjecture nor supposition, but a stark reality, that believers are the *watchful-eye* to communities which embody conflicts and confusions. Through the eyes of faith, this *light* must shine into their paths to warn skeptics, cynics and doubters of oncoming onslaughts.

Amidst the standings of both religious and secular lifestyles, lie realities which require an eye to see beyond the horizon of conflicts. These views will reveal the assurances of peace in the midst of conflicts, optimism in the times of chaos and growth in the midst of baroness. Because of the opportunity of filtering forward progression out of chaos, people everywhere, but especially those of the Faith Community, ought to be vigilant. As expected, faith seeing eyes must continue to unveil silver-lines in life's darkened clouds.

Some might think that they are a part of a Faith Community while simultaneously dwelling elsewhere; be it socially, morally, practically or emotionally. Making the flip-flop from family to foe brings along much trappings and conflicts. Unfortunately, there is hardly a time when being "torn between lovers" has proven to be healthy for the betrothed. Remember, *"No one can serve two masters." (Luke 16:13 NLT).*

Some find it challenging to keep up to this standard, when they are seeing *"through a glass dimly" (1 Corinthians 13:12).* In spite of struggles to shine in a darkened world, those who desire to see clearly are to be reminded that great help is available. When their spiritual sight becomes blurred, it can be reclaimed through spiritual centering. Regular Bible reading and studies will refresh clear foster on their faith-stories. Prayer and supplication will enact submission of self-will unto the will of God. Fasting and consecrations will bring renewed strength to overcome conflicts. Singing Psalms and spiritual hymns will lift inner spirits to a realm of praise and thanksgiving unto God and Spiritual centering will give strength to those who desire to withstand sensual and spiritual conflicts.

Sensual appeals to the glitters and glamour of the world's goods oftentimes spark spiritual conflicts. Sensuality is like a taste of splendor to the tongue, stimulating words to the earlobes, dazzling articles to the eyes, breathtaking fragrances to the nostrils and as velvet when touched. Sensuality entraps both those with twisted minds and those of good intentions, leaving the likes to testify of the victim's perils.

Cravings for the world's goods can be irresistible and fictitiously invigorating, often urging a person to try a sample and wedging conflicts and suspicion in the mind. Unfortunately, samples become insufficient, and then cravings and urges for more of these delights compel the sampler to step into counterfeit pleasures. Their preferences for more of these delights, rather than that which glorifies the Creator, often grow to more of the same.

Consequently, the sanctified minds suffers defeat, their true *light* goes dim and those who are spiritually impaired find themselves groping in the dark.

Fiery Anointing keeps the imaginary fence around *"the defended cities" (Jeremiah 4:5)*, although many become confused as to the purpose of this fence. This fence is not to keep dwellers from going out of the chosen city, but to protect the city from trespassers. Faith in and focus on the work of Fiery Anointing will enable each sojourner to remain within the safety of the city limits. Only then will those within the defended city can be spared from wolves which shall enter *(Acts 20:29)*.

When Jesus invited Simon Peter and his brother Andrew to be two of His twelve Apostles, He commanded them to follow Him, *"and they straightway left their nets, and followed Jesus" (Matthew 4:19)*. It is noteworthy that after they obeyed and followed Jesus, they continued with Him. Their new-found joy motivated them to serve, endure the taunting because they were of His inner-circle and gave them courage to defend His Gospel, but not without the conflict of returning to catching fishes. Their hope to one day reign with Christ brought them great endurance to see what their end would be. Ministering throughout the then known world, as they invited others to be a part of their newly found Community, brought them joy.

"Contrary to belief, the opportunity to become a part of this Faith

Community did not end with the death of Jesus"[5]. A plan of the rulers of that day was to put an end to 'hope in Jesus', but they did not know that *"He had the keys to* [end the conflict of] *death, Hell and the Grave" (Revelation 1:18).* Since the rulers could not stop Jesus in life, stopping Him by crucifixion became their ultimate objective. To the rulers, creating great doubt and conflict about Jesus' Lord-ship was paramount for their selfish gains, and consequently, falsification of testimonies against Him resulting in his death on the cross. But to their surprise, Jesus' vicarious death provides the single greatest opportunity for humankind to overcome ALL of life's conflict: *"in Me you may have peace. I have conquered the world" (John 16:33 HCSB).*

Because of this, Christendom will forever be challenged to be the shining *light* to those who *"dwell in the land of the shadow of death" (Isaiah 9).* This light must continue to permeate the conflicts of human sensuality, enabling victims to withstand emotional challenges and keep them enjoying emotional harmony. Those who settle for moments of fleeting pleasure elsewhere would hardly know of this calmness, but the purpose of the *light* remains that of illuminating the pathway for life's wandering travelers, so that they might follow Jesus as *"the way"*.

In Jesus' day, Pharisees, Sadducees and Scribes tried to create many conflicts against Him. Knowing their intents, Jesus engaged them in friendly fire, which opened doors for more positive conversations by them. While trapping Jesus was their primary intent, I believe that teaching His followers how to overcome perils of conflicts and entrapments was Jesus' greatest aim. As it was in Jesus' day, legalism and the dogmas are still being used to create continue confusion, but those who desire to resist conflicts, can enjoy life in the pleasures of friendly fire. Take a second look, when necessary, to see what is good amidst that which is being said by others.

To their questions, *"Which commandment is the most important of them all" (Mark 12:30 ISV),* Jesus gave an insightful answer to His critic; for it was equally important for Him to have answered tactfully and truthfully. His careful and tactful reply disarmed His critics and diverted them from continuing with their form of entrapment. As Jesus demonstrated tact when working through conflicts, a similar approach ought to be followed. Remember, *"a soft answer turneth away wrath: but grievous words stir up anger" (Proverbs 15:1).* Leave off conflicts until tomorrow!

Impending conflicts by the lawyer who asked Jesus for guidance to salvation also became a moment for Him to engage them into friendly fire. As the lawyer attempted to justify himself, he soon reverted to his self-righteousness by asking, *"Who is my neighbor?" (Luke 10:29 NIV).* Through the Parable of the Good Samaritan, Jesus points out that an indigent person is *neighbor.* Nothing in this parable points to the needy person as being neither an associate nor a group member to the Good Samaritan. In fact, the needy person was not a Samaritan, but a *Jewish man (v30).*

Jews did not have dealings with Samaritans, but the one in this parable needed and received help from a *'Samaritan Dog'*. Samaritan, Canaanites, Syrians, and Phoenicians were outcast: *"Go nowhere among the Gentiles" (Matthew 10:5 ESV)*. Clearly, the *Jew* was not off the same community as the Good Samaritan. Being neighborly includes showing care to persons who are uncomfortably different; a good neighbor shows compassion, hence removing the conflict of class-struggles.

Compassion is a word which summarizes two verses from Matthew chapter five: *"Ye have heard ... thou shalt love thy neighbour, and hate thine enemy. But I say unto you, Love your enemies"*. Compassion is a measure of willingness to spark friendly fires amidst chaos. Persons who look, think, speak and behave differently should never be marginalized. *True light* gives off rescue signal to those who are experiencing conflicts.

So *Love your neighbor as yourself (Matthew 19:19)*. Building relationship with others is secondary only to loving God. No longer should there be demarcations to the exclusion of those of other nationalities, economic statuses, color, race, gender, geographical regions, educational status or associations.
Demarcations must no longer be seen as a tool for marginalization of persons who are not similar in faith, heritage or social standings. Resisting these conflicts across these wide gulfs might seem impossible of oneself, but sharing *Agape (G)* kind of love will embrace those who appear to be different. *Agape* love elevates the

disenfranchised to enjoy communal kindness through friendly fire and friendly fire must transcend to those who are not a part of "the inner circle".

At best, humankind is a depraved and fallen victim from grace, undeserving of kindness, but there remains the duty to spark friendly fire and resist conflicts.

Therefore, I charge you to:-
1. Kindle friendly fire.
2. Discard score sheets and allow Fiery Anointing to permeate misguidance.
3. Discourage conflicts.
4. Avoid actions, behaviors and thoughts, which can escalate to conflicts.
5. Resist conflicts, they can be one's greatest enemy.
6. Maintain a Christ-centered lifestyle.
7. Live to assimilate the good aspects of others through friendly fire.
8. Never allow personal desires to be a priority at the expense of the well-being of another.
9. Make a commitment to love others as self and demonstrate this notion through speech, deeds and actions.
10. Remember, neighbors are not those in the inner-circle, but those who are in need.

"All things both in heaven and in earth were created by GOD: be

they visible or invisible, thrones or dominions, principalities or powers. He is before all things, the head of the body and He has preeminence in all things." (Colossians 1:16-18).

-3-

FIERY TRIALS

In human experiences, crisis refers to an emotional distress which arises from a situational development or social source. A crisis usually creates a temporary helplessness to cope with the situation at hand, it does not last long, it is self-limiting and it is manifested in many different forms. Crisis cannot be resolved by the usual problem-solving methods of its victim and intervention is usually a short-term helping process. While some crises resolutions take longer than others, those which are not resolved within the usually short timeframe develop into conflict episode.

Decades ago, Freud laid a foundation showing that humankind is a complex being, capable of self-discovery and change. He suggested that most of the conflicts which adult grapple with are direct results of negative childhood experiences[6]. Whereas Freud's work focused on disturbed individuals, From (1941), Maslow (1970), and Erikson (1963) did much to lay a basis for crisis theories. They believed that a "specially challenged" person is abnormal. Normalcy was defined as having all mental, physical and cognitive faculties in place.

In every facet of life, there are varied types and degrees of crisis which oftentimes grow into conflicts. Conflicts are present in every kind of relationships: husband / wife, parent / child-ren, employer / employee, clergy / laity, or teacher / student.

Seemingly, conflicts dominate human activities in every facet of living and in every arena of civilization. While social conflicts are devastating to relationships, conflicts in some civic arenas seem to fuel the ego of the players for a season. One can hardly imagine sereneness in a political arena; seemingly, while some participants achieve political success through conflicts, others are crushed.

Agon {ag-one'} (G) - is the root word for conflict. Some synonyms for agon are fight, contention, wrestle and adversity. Strife, dissimulation and schisms are primary agents of conflicts, each having the potential to create tensions within relationships and among group members. Conflict amidst Christians is spiritual warfare. Warfare can be emotional, mental or physical, with the earliest recording being between "Cain and Abel" (Genesis 4:1-15). Able, a shepherd had no problem parting with the best of his flocks, for the physical things merely created a transient mode to him. On the other hand, Cain, a farmer, wrestled with physicality of his day; his acquisitions were more important to him than the life of his brother.

Not only did Cain struggled with knowing that his brother was unselfish towards the Giver of all things, but he grappled with giving God his best sacrifice. Unfortunately for Cain, who begrudged his brother, he was unable to see the world as his transient and temporal abode. Thousands of years later, the world is still a place of fleeting pleasures not worthy of God's notice and humankind continues to strive for passing gains, rather than building lasting relationships. As it was amidst the first nuclear family, conflicts continue to prove that they are catastrophic, sparing none who thinks that they can overcome them by their own volition. *"Then the LORD said to Cain, "Where is Abel your brother?" He said, "I do not know; am I my brother's keeper?" (Genesis 4:9 NAS).*

The first nuclear family was close to being perfect prior to Cain's homicidal actions. Like many today, this family was not spared from fiery trials by the enemy of the souls. This enemy continues to live up to its repudiation of the innocents, driving wedges of jealousy and bitterness between the best of relationships. Conflicts stop short of nothing before breathing disgrace, destruction, humiliation and finally death upon victims. If allowed, conflicts will ruffle the neatest package of grace, rip apart the tightest wrapping of a sanctified life and sentence victims to live in slums of shame and spiritual debaucheries.

Conflicts have legions of disguises. They can appear as open clashes between individuals or groups, moods of incompatible feelings, hostile promotions of opposing ideas or as opposite forces between ideas of common interests. To the indifferent person, hearing a simple "good morning" from another can bring on conflict. One can hardly be surprise how often conflicts oppose order, defy Biblical governance and create tensions for those giving services unto God and to His people. Conflicts lurk near to every solemn thought, action or good deed; with a readiness to dash the spirit of harmony and with the anxiety to destroy every good thought and every good deed. *"When I would do good, evil is present with me" (Romans 7:21).*

With individuals, conflicts bring about inward warring of the soul, which can be accompanied with outward battles. The "Man of the 20th Century", A. J. Tomlinson, shares in one of his books that his yearning for a Fiery Anointing experience was his "greatest conflict"[7]. He desired Fiery Unction as he led the Church of God through her formidable years. Because he struggled to obtain a pure heart, he was denied the experience of Fire Baptism for a time, but his yearning to overcome impurities was eventually replaced with The Gift. Believing that this Anointing would be his greatest ally, Tomlinson soon testified of speaking in several unknown tongues, upon receiving his Pentecost.

When misguided by *"the lust of the eye, the lust of the flesh and the pride of life" (1 John 2:16),* persons step out of bounds and *"sow to their flesh" (Galatians 6:8).* Firstly, this inward warring brings about fierce hindrances to these individuals. Secondarily, these hindrances are passed on to family systems, then into our communities and workplace. Several generators of relational conflicts for readers to consider are 1) pride, 2) beguiling, 3) jealousy, 4) strife and pretending.

1. Pride lurks wherever people coexist and is common manifestation of those desiring to show that others are in error,

when in fact they themselves are the guilty persons. This warring between the flesh and the Spirit creates conflicts both with self and with others. A first-line of defense for proud-prowlers is the habit of telling half-truth/untruth in an attempt to camouflage the real issues. Pride becomes a deadly force with a determination not to be exposed; pretending that truth and deceit are one and the same.

When the proud is convicted by Fiery Anointing, *"the accuser of the brothers and sisters" (Revelation 12:10 NLT),* would either retreat or continue to fight with the intentions to severely ruin the good testimonies of victims. Pride is firstly divisive to its bearer, then secondarily destructive to all who come into its path; it is NOT a respecter of person. *"Every kingdom divided against itself is brought to desolation; and every city or house divided against itself shall not stand" (Matthew 12:25).*

Pride is a scorner, bringing strife and reproach with it, *(Proverb 22:10).* This is a rather strong statement but very true; it is God's word. Scorning of another is not a portrait of God's nature: *"God is not a God of confusion, but of peace" (1 Corinthians 14:33).* All are fearfully and wonderfully made in God's likeness and image. Scorning is a form of pushing others away, as the scorner purposely become un-relational.

Scorning which suggests a 'better than' opinion of self to that of another brings imbalances to relationships. Scorning is open and unqualified dislike, disapproval and disregard, rejection of another, refusal of another with contempt or disdain. Pride transfers the proud out of the group which desires to have '*all things common*' and places them into special-interest groups as self-importance, stuck-up, arrogant and conceited. Haughtiness, arrogance and conceit are synonyms of pride. *"Disgrace is before ruin and pride of spirit before misfortune" (Proverbs 16:18 AR).*

2. The homeostasis of a group is often changed into cunning beguiling of fellow members, who have a hunger to achieve personal agenda at all cost. Some would seek to advance their plans at the price of disregarding those whom they claim that they want to serve; "Throwing out the baby with the bath water". At times, they behave as though there is something for them to prove among their fellow group-members. They believe that they must do or say something which would help them to gain grounds or get ahead of the pack. The idea of getting ahead of the pack creates sub-interest in the group. This ideology becomes a dis-service to the group when such a person is not serving as resources for the edification of the group.

Beguiling shows-up wherever and whenever the principals for harmony are ignored; *"agree with one another so that there may be no divisions among you" (1 Corinthians 1:10 NIV).* The realization that earthly gains are temporal and spiritual rewards are eternal is a way to take a grip of the "*no division in the body*" mandated. Because all are working for the same *"daily wage" (Matthew 20:2),* gains are minuscule when they are realized through beguiling. No, these are not principals of yester-years; harmonious blessings are promise to all who resist temptations to hoax fellow group members.

3. As jealousy strained relationships in the beginning, jealousy continues its onslaught. Group members working in unison to achieve a preferred future ought to be the underlining purpose of their common group; to this, members ought to agree that there is no-place for jealousy among them. Jealousy promotes murmuring, disputing and division; as was exhibited by Lot towards Abraham. Although Abraham was committed to dwell in the unity of peace which God established within his house, Abraham's covenanted relationship with God did not stop the infestation of Lot's jealous rages. Abram, a mature father and an unselfish leader, stood his grounds and decreed: not today! *"Let there be no strife" (Genesis 13:8 DBT).*

Similarly, membership by covenant does not preclude jealousy among group members, but jealousy is often manifested through group members who are not willing to prefer others before self. Too often, group leaders are pressed to settle commotions of group members, who, like Lot, desire to follow ways which seem right in their eyes. Therefore, it becomes necessary for leaders to take counsel in an approach by James, *the Lord's brother,* who went down the middle of the road while addressing the problem of contention in the church of his day. *"... quarrels and fights come from the evil desires at war within you" (James 4:1-2 NLT)* was his admonition.

Overseer James identifies wickedness and jealousy as root causes of destructive intentions in the early church. Like the early church which was comprised of members from one extreme to another, those who believe that they were gifted with Fiery Anointing and nominal members, continue to remain agents of warfare within common group. Although they fight and engage in conflicts which they deem necessary to satisfy appointed positions and selfish urges, yet they come up unfulfilled. What is the need for jealousy? Believers are the head and not the tail, lenders and not borrowers, possessors of authority to stomp-out all forms of jealousy and to subdue all appearances of the prince of the air.

4. Strife is something which is conjured up by the sensual mind, thus making it an active component of the works of the flesh *(Galatians 5:20 NIV)*. Too often, persons who should be committed to spirituality, allow strife to blemish their good works. Strife exposed relational shortcomings and brings on fighting and wrestling. As the natural mind grows envious, then separated from spiritual harmony *(1 Corinthians 3:3),* the spirit-man needs to retreat into times of refreshing and self-restoration.

Individuals who are *sober and vigilant* are more fitting to constrain themselves from engaging in strife and fighting of the moment; their spiritual maturity becomes the enabler to resist temptation.

Oftentimes, brawlers find joy in an occasion to take part in strife, when they are either enticed by others or if they engage themselves. Since unfriendly fire disrupts harmony, all must resist strife and show good examples, in order that they might convince others to lay down war-tools; a good example is infinitely better than a convincing sermon or an earth-shattering testimony.

5.	Pretenders, hypocrites: *pollute (H)*, of piety can be as lethal as brawlers. When translated, derivatives of this Hebrew word are godless, profane and wicked. Some synonyms for hypocrisy are sanctimonious, bigotry and bad faith. Hypocrisy is dissimulation, stage acting and double-dealing, all of which bring ruin to wholesome relationships. In the context of a group, two common forms of hypocrisy are "back-dooring" leadership and "two-timing" fellow members. Back-dooring is when a member discredits leadership, while at the same time pretending that they are supporting leadership. Two-timing is when a member pretends to be a friend with another member, but is simultaneously discrediting the would-be friend. *"Don't just pretend to love others" (Romans 12:9 NLT).*

Jesus rebuked the rulers of the Synagogue because of their hypocrisy towards a woman whom He healed. These rulers staged the ill-health of a woman as an opportunity to attack Jesus. They took issues with Jesus for healing a woman, who was sick for eighteen years *(Luke 13:16),* on the Sabbath day. Although they were hardly concerned about keeping the Sabbath, they justified their cunning craftiness with the disguise of keeping the Sabbath Holy. Sadly, these same rulers were satisfied with customs and traditions which compromised the keeping of the Sabbath, when the concessions were gainful to them: *"they* [untied] *their ox from the stall, and lead them away to watering" (v15)*.

While the needs of the woman exceeded those of oxen, the rulers showed insensitivity towards her, *"a seed of Abraham"*. Had it been one of the rulers of the temple needing liberation after *eighteen years,* perhaps the entire sect would have sought-out help for him, on the Sabbath Day. Therefore, it was hypocritical for the rulers to oppose healing for a *"daughter of Abraham" (v16)*, in pretense of defending of the Sabbath. The truth is, those rulers lacked sincerity for the woman's wellbeing. After all, the Sabbath was made for (wo)/man!   (Matthew 2:27).

Enemies of conflicts have not changed their plans to *"kill, steal and to destroy" (John 10:10 MASB)*; they continue to be the *"enemy of the soul" (Psalm 143:3):* never ceasing to let up or to slow down their onslaught. Some recommendations against their prowling among group members are:-

1. Remain joined together by purpose and stand for truth and right *"against the wiles of the enemy" (Ephesians 6:11)*.

2. Dwell in righteousness and do not become distracted by pastimes which do not bring value to the common purpose.

3. Whereas solutions by the psychologist and sociologist are acceptable ways to resolve conflicts, Scripture dictate methods by which brethren should resolve problems. As it was necessary for the early church, having *"all things common" (Acts 2:44)* is a great anecdote.

4. Remain keepers one-to-another and holistic spiritual bonds will be formed. Respecting each other.

No longer should persons be satisfied knowing that they share in weakness common to former greats: *"I do not do the good I want, but the evil I do not want is what I keep on doing" (Romans 7:19 ESV)*. Conflict can be as subtle as eating and drinking that which are pleasing to the eyes, but consumption of the same might not be expedient for the body at a said time. Turning away from these foods and drinks would be a victory over temptation, and when this *thorn in the flesh* is brought under subjection, persons can shout with joy: "Thank God, I made it over!"

All can be empowered to rise above conflicts by the warmth from the Anointing Fires. When this affection is absent from the lives of individuals, low self-esteem can raise its ugly head. A clue of victory is being ready to give words of praise rather than being anxious to receive words of kindness or expressions of commendations. Extolling others provide flint-like sparks, which are necessary for friendly fire. Here are some helps to follow when conflict fire is burning in the hearts of members and leaders.

1. When protection from infractions is allowed, safeguard against the veracity of strife is equally near.

2. If ever become embellished in strife, meekness allows tolerance and is a lifter-up above them all.

3. When He bares up the brokenhearted, unlimited strength will be available as endurance over the worst offerings of others.

4. When conversations take unpredictable turns for the worst and sparks of surprise ignite conflict fires, "see no evil, hear no evil, speak no evil".

5. Regardless of the circumstances, hospitality will keep conflicts in check.

6. Move swiftly to *"restore such an one in the spirit of meekness" (Galatians 6:1-2).*

7. When conversations become testy, repulsive or offensive and a way of escape is needed away from the moment, remember that the fight is against principalities.

8. Use good spiritual judgment, especially when the stage is set for persons to exert zeal in ways which will bring additional offences: *"Let your speech be always with grace, seasoned with salt, that ye may know how ye ought to answer every man" (Colossians 4:6).*

9. Identifying the root-cause of conflicts is hardly a natural process, but spiritually discerned. *"The beginning of strife is as when one letteth out water: therefore leave off contention, before it be meddled with" (Proverb 17:14).*

10. Fiery anointing is the greatest keeper and defender. If strife is not left-off when He points the way to the door of escape, He will allow the individuals to fend for self. When He hints, leave-off strife immediately.

11. *"Avoid foolish questions, and genealogies, and contentions, and strivings about the law; for they are unprofitable and vain" (Titus 3:9).*

12. Conflicts become more potent if unresolved. When necessary do not hesitate to seek clarification from others.

13. Let crisis intervention be a process of weeding-out root-causes, and restoring of good fate. The use of external conciliator is a Biblical mandate, but do not violate the Biblical pattern.

14. When the need arises, work along with counselors who are not novices.

15. *"Dare any of you, having a matter against another, go to law before the unjust, and not before the saints? Do ye not know that the saints shall judge the world? And if the world shall be judged by you, are ye unworthy to judge the smallest matters?*

Know ye not that we shall judge angels?" (1 Corinthians 6:1-3).

-4-

DOUSING THE FIRE.

Consider this epilog by The Apostle Paul:

"Finally, my brethren, be strong in the Lord, and in the power of his might. Put on the whole armour of God, that ye may be able to stand against the wiles of the devil. For we wrestle not against flesh and blood, but against principalities, against powers, against the rulers of the darkness of this world, against spiritual wickedness in high places. Wherefore take unto you the whole armour of God, that ye may be able to withstand in the evil day, and having done all, to stand. Stand therefore, having your loins girt about with truth, and having on the breastplate of righteousness; And your feet shod with the preparation of the gospel of peace; Above all, taking the shield of faith, wherewith ye shall be able to quench all the fiery darts of the wicked. And take the helmet of salvation, and the sword of the Spirit, which is the word of God. Praying always with all prayer and supplication in the Spirit, and watching thereunto with all perseverance and supplication for all saints" (Ephesians 6:10-18).

Though people everywhere are trapped by either spiritual or sensual warfare, all can be overcomers if they would put on the whole armour which the Lord Himself has prepared. Arm forces personnel put on full amour at the beginning of their work shift and take it off at shift's end. Likewise, all who desire protection from the conflicts of life ought to put on "the whole armour" throughout their faith-walk.

Methodia, (G), is translated as standing in defense of the methods of conflicts, although the enemy comes after each one differently. A single attack on a lone individual will hardly have a fatal impact on their faith community or family systems, but attacks from different prospective on multiple individuals within the community can severely threaten the group's survival.

Every community member must have confidence to stand firmly in opposition to conflicts and avoid becoming a part thereof. Satan is the prince of the air, but it is the Lord Himself who rules the universe and all of the forces which can adversely affect His chosen people. Therefore, believers must abide in Him if they are going to stand victoriously against these forces. Amidst these painful persuasions, unfortunate circumstances can befall the most sincere person, as well as the most influential leader; not even Martin Luther was spared.

It was "the greatest hymn of the greatest man of the greatest period of German history" the "Battle Hymn of the Reformation"[8] which brought comfort to those imprisoned for supporting Luther's religious vision. Centuries later, this hymn symbolizes some of the greatest victories by individuals today, to abide in the secret place of the Most High. More importantly, it is a resounding resolve that there is victory at the end of every battle for those who desire to remain clothed in the armour of God.

In 1720, a remarkable revival began in a town in Moravia, and when Jesuits opposed it, the meetings were prohibited. Those who assembled themselves in rebellion were seized and imprisoned in stables and cellars. At David Nitschmann's house, where a hundred and fifty persons gathered, which the police broke into and seized the bibles, hymnals and other books which they were using. Not dismayed, the group struck up this stanza from the great Battle Hymn.

> *"And though this world, with devils filled,*
> *Should threaten to undo us;*
> *We will not fear, for God hath willed*
> *His truth to triumph through us".*[9]

From similar event, the Protestant Reformation flowed through the new-found conviction of Martin Luther's: *"the just shall live by faith"*. To Luther, the righteous were able to overcome unjust threatening and frustrations, because they trusted in the fulfillment of the promises of God. Many of Luther's followings were held as prisoners, but they believed that God had willed His truth in them. Even when they did not understand, God was their sovereign Lord through their new found faith in Him. Their confidence and hope remained fixed that God was not going to abandon them. Simply put, they did not give up their fame to walk by faith for the disdain of being held hostage by unbelief. Imprisonment for trusting in God's word could not stop them from believing in Him.

Adversaries never get enough of their foes. People think of the Devil and very real people think of demons. It will not be strange meeting someone who testifies that they saw the Devil, although this person might be thought of as crazy. Everybody talks about the devil and his demons. Think for a moment of a demon that controls a bad habit in a person's life. Real people want to know how to shun 'the adversary, the devil'. The adversary is that which brings about chaos, while destroying normalcy and harmony. Because of demonic powers, harmonious relationships are busted, lives are crushed, good health of persons take flight and mental stabilities become a thing of the past.

As it was in the beginning, it is hardly possible to see with the natural eyes the readiness of the enemy of the soul. Most scholars, who possess Biblical persuasions regarding spiritual warfare, agree that their weaponry is ready to be used to the detriment of humankind. Their loaded canons are ready to be used to destroy the likes of successful businesses, civic organizations, wholesome homes, striving auxiliaries and progressive religious groups.

Glaring bayonets are blinding the natural eyes from seeing the loaded bombers. They are ready to release their artillery against human targets of every race, creed, ethnicity, religious persuasions and social background. Like the warrior's noise, the enemy does a super job distracting its prey. Because enemies' purpose is for their prey to be unaware of their forward progress, preys are forever shunning their distractions and artilleries to destroy them.

The enemy knows pertinent information about their prey; name, background, likes and dislikes, weaknesses and strengths. Because the enemy continues to study its prey, the enemy's vulnerability is often a surprise. Destroying believers, thus silencing their testimonies, is the enemy's single focus day and night. All experience the same threats whether they are spiritually fit or emotionally weak, bold or shy, serious or casual bible students, well or poorly educated, widowed, single, divorced, man or woman, belonging to a group or a lone-ranger. Be it known today, the enemy is not a respecter of person.

Do not think it strange to read that "the prince of the air" tries to share dwelling space with real people. Since his plan is to kill, steal and destroy, he sneaks into the heart and mind of persons who entertains him. He is the prince of the air; therefore, his movements are only confined by the atmosphere and by the Prince of Peace. One's every step is stalked and at times disillusioned, telling oneself that the mare existence of the enemy is not all together true. Thinking of the enemy in an exaggerated manner means that the mission of the enemy is already bolstered. Putting it simple, the enemy wants to spiritually cripple every foe and bring about their demise, causing them to plummet into ruin.

Paul begins this epilog with the admonition to *"be strong in the Lord, and in the power of his might" (v10)*. It is unlikely that humankind will be guided by the spirit each and every moment. Therefore, knowledge of the enemy is important, when humankind is unable to discern the enemies' schemes. To the contrary, most have never studied the strategies of the enemy, who wants real people to think nothing of its plans of attack. In fact, if more people seek to know the will of God for their lives, they would know more about the enemies' desire for them. Yes, as the enemy continues to become exposed, foes will find out that the enemy cannot stand in the power of Fiery Anointing. Since involuntary exposure of the enemy is not an admissible reason to be ignorant, destruction is ahead for those who lack knowledge *(Hosea 4:6)*.

Like the armor of arm forces personnel, the Christian armour is made to be worn and should not be put off until warfare has been completed. Believers are commanded to: *"Put on the whole armour of God, that ye may be able to stand against the wiles of the devil"* (v11). Combat is not against other individuals, a person's own corrupt nature or the evil deceit of others. The enemy has thousands of ways of beguiling the very best of humankind, but the ultimate fight is against an enemy of the soul.

"We wrestle not against flesh and blood, but against principalities, against powers, against the rulers of the darkness of this world, against spiritual wickedness in high places" (v12). The enemy assaults the things which the soul takes pleasure in and works overtime to deface the heavenly images of our minds. Without a doubt, all must decide by God's grace, not to yield to Satan, but instead, to resist him. *"Resist the devil, and he will flee from you" (James 4:7).* Satan gains ground whenever there is as much as a

slight yielding, such as doubt in kindred spirit among group members, doubt in the integrity of leadership or doubt in the whole armour.

The safest haven from life's conflicts is beneath the armour: *"Take unto you the whole armour of God, that ye may be able to withstand in the evil day"* (v13). Since the armour does not cover the back, turning back in the fight for God and right is not an option. Turning back is less of a chance for the individual who submits to the whole armour. There is no need to fear, doubt or question God's instruction to march forward in victory, as the prophets of old affirm. *"Fear thou not; for I am with thee: be not dismayed; for I am thy God" (Isaiah 41:10).*

Truth is most vital to the whole armour of God and the girdle which cannot be negotiated nor can it be fabricated. *"Stand therefore, having your loins girt about with truth"* (v14a). Jesus is truth, He is life *(John 14:6),* He who does not change *(Hebrews 13:8),* He who overcomes the world *(John 16:33),* He who could not be kept down by death nor the grave *(Luke 18:13)* and He who will return one day to receive those who know truth unto Himself *(John 14:3).*

Neither intellectualism nor arrogance by those who think that they have gained great scholastic knowledge is Truth. A 'saying' by an individual is truth only by the standard of that individual. A good book might not be Truth although it might be written by the best of authors. Truth is The Bible, God's inspired Word. Truth is brighter than the blazing sun and higher than the Rocky Mount; hence, nothing can be compared to it. Truth does not have imposters, since it is *"Wonderful, Counsellor, The mighty God, The everlasting Father, The Prince of Peace" (Isaiah 9:6).*

If the prince of darkness can get a person to abandon Truth, their end is eminently near. Because his plan is to ultimately destroy the soul of humankind, whatever he says and thinks is cunning craftiness. Tricking persons into disobeying Truth is Satan's most potent tool, but *"if (Truth) be for us, who can be against us?" (Romans 8:31).* Neither peril, tribulation, distress, persecution, famine, nakedness nor sword cannot change truth. When counted as *"sheep for the slaughter" (v36),* be persuaded that *"death, nor life, angels, nor principalities nor powers, things present nor things to come, height nor depth, nor any other creature, shall be able to separate us from* (truth)*" (v38-v39).* Truth rocks!

Truth separates saint from sinners, wheat from tears, and the bound from the free. Truth makes sinner to forsake their ways, the sexual promiscuous to return home and warriors to lay down their war tools. Truth makes the drug addicts to give up their turn for another "hit"; declaring, "there is not a high like the Most High"! Truth changes discord to times of peace, strengthens the weak instead of flinging them to the wolves of confusion, and builds up the babe in Christ instead of pitching them out with the bath-water. Truth will break self-will and bring supporters to follow to leadership as they are led by Fiery Anointing. Truth stops strife and schisms at the door, barring them out for evermore!

The greatest combat manual ever written is Truth, declaring believers as the composition of the only army that is promised victory before the first shot is to be fired. Power is guaranteed by Truth, over the world's conflicts and victory over the conflict of social ills. The unemployed and the downtrodden can have hope, as Truth redirects them away from welfare systems. Truth says: *"The LORD shall make thee the head, and not the tail; and thou shalt be above only, and thou shalt not be beneath" (Deuteronomy 28:13).*

To those who are struggling in economic conflicts, truth says you will have houses which you did not build and vineyards which you did not plant: *"a sinner's wealth is stored up for the righteous" (Proverbs 13:22).* As economic woes blind the eyes from economic recovery, there is nothing which is too hard for the Master who calms every raging storm. Social ills might be the consequence of economic tumult but He who is maker of heaven and earth holds the keys to success. Truth is the guarantor over rejection; therefore, believers of Truth are not and will not be defeated.

Truth says endure hardness as a good soldier, speak up in the spirit of peace, stand up in the armour as a soldier of the cross and be that which Truth declares you to be: *"a chosen generation, a royal priesthood, an holy nation, a peculiar people"* (1 Peter 2:9). Because Truth says that the Father will give all that is asked of Him *(John 16:23),* all can expect that their enemy of confusion will eventually be bound.

Integrity which dictates to humankind how to live and how to relate one to another is Truth: put *"away lying, speak every man truth with his neighbour: for we are members one of another" (Ephesians 5:25).* Therefore, all must make it a practice to live honestly and truthfully. One who lies stand in agreement with the father of all lies. Hardly can the one who practices lying stand against the enemy who spoke the very first lie and continues lying ever since.

Knowing what Truth says about conflict resolution is confidence that every conflict can be resolved. *"No weapon that is formed against thee shall prosper; and every tongue that shall rise against thee in judgment thou shalt condemn." (Isaiah 54:17).* As it was with *'God's chosen people',* the Israelites, Truth is on the side of all who might be under siege by confusion. *"Fear ye not, stand still, and see the salvation of the LORD" (Exodus 14:13).* Truth endures to the end!

"Stand; ...... having on the breastplate of righteousness" (v14b). Righteousness that is accorded to believers is the breastplate against the enemy's conflicts. When Christ's virtues are implanted into individuals, their hearts are fortified against the enemy's plans

and their lifestyle will only be congruent with right-living, if they are yielding to Christ. Although it is for the asking once an individual is a new creature, right-living requires daily nurturing. The righteous are those who possess and practice godly characters and virtues. Righteous people live faultlessly before God and fellow believers, although they are accused on many fronts.

Who may dwell in your sanctuary?
Who may live on your holy hill?
He whose walk is blameless
(Psalm 15 NIV).

Those dabbling in the enemy's games of making confusion should not be surprise when adverse conditions come to their dwellings. Sowing discord, creating division and being disruptive to progress are signs of an unrighteous heart. God hears all who ask forgiveness, but dipping in-and-out of unrighteousness is not a worthy risk to take. Those who believe that they can "flirt with the enemy" must be reminded that they shall reap that which they sow *(Galatians 6:7).* There will be either corruption from the flesh or life eternal life from the Spirit.

Be assured, the character assassin will return to a house of slander. Malice will yield cruelty, hatred and untimely death, begrudges will reap envy and dishonesty will garner deceit. So remember, the breastplate of righteousness protects against spitefulness, the spirit of 'getting even', 'back-dooring' and 'two-timing' of others.

Conflict resolutions are as necessary as graves to the legs. *"Feet shod with the preparation of the gospel of peace", (v15),* will both stand their ground and march forward through fiery trails. Motivation to resist conflicts amidst trials must be drawn from the most sincere knowledge of the gospel. Feet can become a person most important resource, while at the same time, they can be their worst enemy: the Lord hates *"feet that* (is) *swift to mischief" (Proverbs 6:18).*

The feet are for walking and running; therefore forward march must be for good and right. Sometimes, indifferences impair their pathway, but when they reach a place where they cannot move forward any further, they must stand on that which is sure. God's peace is the solid rock which will give sure foothold, but the enemies' way is as shifting sand.

"Take the shield of faith, wherewith ye shall be able to quench all the fiery darts of the wicked" (v16). The shield is a defensive weapon of protection and faith is an essential, not an incidental. There must be confidence in the shield, in order for one to be protected by it. Wavering of one's belief opens a hole through which the enemy pours doubt. All defenses are meaningless without the confidence of faith as a part of the armour. Faith is the 'all-in-all' in the moment of temptation; relying on He who is not seen but He who protects continuously by a shield. When faith is applied through the Word of Truth and the grace of Christ, the flaming arrows of the evil one will be stopped.

One must have faith in order to overcome conflicts! If belief in the armour against contentions and that which we proclaim to stand-up for is absent, we are defeated already. Conflicts are mountainous at times, but faith can remove the largest of them all. Faith says yes when nature says no and declares life when health reports enumerate immediate ends. Faith says paid in full when creditors say payments are delinquent and welcomes the down-trodden when the world-systems condemn them into utter darkness. Faith is the victory! Command the mountain to move and it shall. *(Mark 11:23)*.

Salvation must be the helmet which protects the head from becoming dizzy by the enemy's buzz: *"Take the helmet of salvation" (v17a)*. This good hope of salvation will purify the soul, and keep it from being defiled by Satan. Ultimately deliverance out of spiritual warfare is only possible through Fiery Anointing. Accepting the gift of salvation is what makes individuals different from their enemy. Salvation gives an added layer of protection against feuding, schisms and indifferences. A helmet assures soundness of mind and a sound mind produces love and power to overcome struggles. This helmet assures the bearer that the loins of their mind will remain protectively wrapped up, regardless of what the enemy tries.

To be fully armed for battle defense, the defensive weapon, *"the sword of the Spirit, which is the word of God" (v17b)* is a must to have. All are reminded, by the word of God that the sword protects who-so-ever-will from the prowls of conflicts. This sword subdues and mortifies blasphemous thoughts, unbelief and errors, as they assault from without. A single text, when understood and correctly applied, destroys a temptation or an objection, subduing the most formidable adversary. Jesus quoted the written Word repeatedly to the tempter, "it is written", and the tempter left for a season.

Those who desire to be victorious must be armed with the sword of the Spirit and must know how to use the Word both offensively and defensively. Having to rely solely upon others for defense by the sword of the spirit is not sufficient. Spiritual leaders, family members or friends will not always be adequately near, as defense from the enemy is needed. Should there be a need to maneuver quickly, each individual must understand how to operate the sword and know how to quickly remove it from its sheath. Rightfully enacting the sword, in the moment, will make the Word of God effective *(Hebrews 4:12)*.

A most effective application of the Sword is through *"praying always with all prayer and supplication in the Spirit, and watching thereunto with all perseverance and supplication for all saints" (v18)*. Prayer gives mobility to all of the parts of the armour. There are many duties of religion in each respective station, but in-earnest prayer must precede them all for best results. Though set and solemn, prayer may not seem seasonable when other duties are required; yet, short pious prayers darted out always bring strength.

Earnest prayer gives direction to and puts the seeker into direct intimacy with God.

Holy thoughts must be center stage in believer's every-day activities, in order that they do not harvest an empty prayer. In-earnest prayer can be in public, private, secret, communal, solitude, sober or sudden. As one of the four Benedictine *Lectio divina* stages defines, prayer must include confession of sins. Prayer must express total dependence on God, both in petitioning for mercy and giving thanks. It can be traditional, through the reading of Scripture, with icons, in tongues, in the midst of conflict or in times of peace. Communion with God is more important than the style of prayer used to reach Him.

Perseverance in prayer is required, in spite of conflicts or in any other hindrances, both for self and for others. The enemies are mighty and humankind is without strength, especially when they refuse to pray in supplication. By the power and might of God, all can be overcomers; therefore, all must stir up themselves and cry out, as the Psalmist, and seek him diligently *(Psalm 63:1-2).*

God's armour is His protective covering for His faithful and it allows these believers to withstand the schemes and conflicts of life. The enemy is brilliant in ways of deception, cunning in ways of making mockeries, relentless in fights and knows what it takes to bring humankind to their knees. Since believers are *"not ignorant of his schemes" (2 Corinthians 2:11),* victory is theirs.

Be strong by standing in the strength of the Prince of Peace and remain alert to the tricks of the enemy. Many succeed because they took cover under God's armour and all who put confidence in this armour will overcome the onslaught of conflicts which are taking the *kingdom* by force. *(Matthew 11:12).*

To be an overcomer, keep a right attitude towards winning the fight and start the day in prayer. "Lord this is your day and I cannot walk in it by my own strength. I cannot withstand the challenges which it brings and I lack the know-how to win battles in my strength. I cannot protect myself, so I give you my mind, my emotions and my will. Please make me yours again. I give you thanks for victory to overcome challenges of this day".

So fight and be brave against all evil,
Never run, nor ever lag behind;
If you would win for God and the right,
Just keep on the firin' line[10]

-5-

TAKE OUT THE LOG

A catch-phrase for stage acting is the hypocrite's decree. So then, what generates the winds beneath the wings of the phony? Many persons have made pretense the default way of living. Instead of being sober and honest in their conversations, conflicting messages are passed on from one to the other. Be it the lone ranger or persons of any group or community, Scriptural mandate to this vast crowd is to get rid of hypocrisy *(1Peter 2:1 ISV)*.

Grace through faith is the enabler for each individual who desires to shun the perils of pretense. When this grace-lifestyle is embraced, letting go of hurt, shame, blame, slander or the spirit to 'get even' becomes easier. Releasing others will begin by *"First get*(ting) *rid of the log in your own eye" (Matthew 7:5 NLT)*. Giving up the 'log' assures transparency and better vision, thus enabling firm stance against hypocrisy.

Relationships will only be harmonious for as long as group members desire to stand against pretense. Guilt of offences in the heart of an individual blurs their vision. Blurred vision distorts the prospective of the beholder from seeing that which is of good report in another person. A seeing-eye-hypocrite is one who is intentionally distorting his own vision of the object or matter at hand. Proverbially speaking, that which blocks clear vision is often larger than that what is to be seen.

A fault can be likened to a small particle in one's eye, yet causing great discomfort. Proportionally, faults can be mote-like particles of dust, as gnat-small flies or as large as logs or boulders. Whenever individuals become victimized by these kinds of irritations, their desire to see the best in others must prevail. Those who are a part of infractions must objectively evaluate themselves first, in order to abstain from making their ideas about others 'laws unto themselves'. Opinions about an infraction will hardly be objective when sited by its victims, since their opinions oftentimes, serve to justify their present disposition. Therefore, villains nor victims are not to be the judge of each other *(Matthew 7:1-2)*.

Never classify an offence of another as little. In spite of the size of the fault, be it as small as a splinter, a mote or a gnat, offences violate the rights of others. Victims will not be at their best emotionally or spiritually, until they are free of the infraction. Too often, the desires of self-centered persons are to magnify the fault in others, in order to hide their own shortcomings. Conversely, true repentance and godly sorrow for one's own faults starts the rooting-out of the log. "It is strange that a man can be in a sinful, miserable condition, and not be aware of it, as that man should have a beam in his eye, and not consider it; but the gods of this world blind the mind. Here is a good rule for reproves: first reform thyself"[11].

Whenever tensions frustrate the will of individuals and influence them to turn away from healthy relationships, the obstructed persons would either launch an attack or seek a way of escape from the perpetrator. Escape can be through denial or by physically running away from the scene. Reflect on those who go as far as taking drastic measures to end their own life, thinking that they would become free from an ordeal or a disappointing experience. In most cases, freedom from this entrapment is as simple as forgiving yourself, with a desire to move forward, since the past cannot be change.

Those who keep their heads in the sand like the ostrich or put on blindfolds like the race horse should be reminded that ignoring conflicts of any kind do not resolve them. The process of ignoring problems serves as an incubator for more severe encounters; ignored problems will burst forth into larger flames. Here are some escape-methods which are often in the vocabulary of many: 'I'm focused on myself', 'I can't take this anymore', 'I don't want to think about this anymore', 'I want to get out of this' and 'It's all about my feelings'. Escapism violates the Biblical principle for conflict resolution: *"restore in meekness, the person who is at fault" (Galatians 6:1).*

Hurting people, who think that they should 'get even', live with the desire to hurt others in return. 'Attack' is a natural response to pain when individuals fail to maintain a 'sanctified mind'. Sensual thoughts of this magnitude will soon render pure minds as undesired places to kindle friendly fire. Whereas people attack one another so as to establish their position of control or manipulation, there is no Biblical support for this. An individual is not to do evil to another because evil was done to them *(Romans 12:17 ISV)*. *"An eye for an eye"* will not promote friendly fire.

The notion of wanting someone to feel pain, just as the pains which were felt during an infraction, places the feelings of the victim as a focal point, but in negative ways. Overcoming evil with good is seldomly the retort, and the preeminence of humility conquers revenges. Group members must grow to the maturity of releasing offenders and letting go of the hurt done to them, through the peace which Jesus gives through His Vicarious death on the cross *(John 14:27 GWT)*.

Simply put, attack methods are hardly pleasant, since they dictate ways which will compound conflicts. Some ways of attack are violence, assault, slander, gossip and litigation. A Leader attacks supporters by spitefully removing them from appointed positions in which they are ably serving. Another way a leader attacks supporters is by failing to appoint a supporter although the supporter is most suited and qualified to serve in a specific role. In either example above, is the leader embattled by the conflict of Nepotism? Is the leader executing vengeance upon the supporter? Is the ideology of the leader one of spite? Whatever is the case, leader ought *"never take revenge" (Romans 12:19)*.

A conscious decision to engage in conflict is showing contempt to the God of all peace. God's grace and truth of His Word is the paths to building friendly-fire amidst conflicts. Do not allow self to fall to the arrogance which fosters the 'get even' form of legalism. An *'eye for an eye'* is the law, but faith-group members are to be reminded that, because their *"life is hid with Christ in God" (Colossians 3:3),* they are to live both by grace and by the laws of God. Grace undergirds the undeserved and fulfills the laws. Mercy justifies doers of the law from well-deserved punishment. Therefore, the group member who is hid with Christ in God is blessed for doing good to them who spites them.

As grace is both unmerited and limitless to all, offended persons should be quick to show mercy instead of reacting to conflicts. They must allow their modesty to reflect the harmony of the Gospel. Showing mercy paves the way for others to see Christ in human-form. Whereas the law enumerates that one should forgive another three times, grace offers the privilege of forgiving another four hundred and ninety times in one day! *(Matthew 18:21-22).*

Biblical principles might appear hard from a humanistic prospective, but the ease of accepting these values can be encouraged through friendly fire. When life is lived in this context, one will often resist sensual things, thus disabling sensual desires from easily taking over. Biblical principles make the process *"easy and light" (Matthew 11: 30 NASB).*

Natural approaches will fuel conflicting behaviors more times than not. The prince of the air creates conflicts and finds countless ways to entice humankind to fall victim to conflicts; therefore, one can hardly give a comprehensive list which should be followed when trying to avoid these hazards. The enemy of the soul is up and down in the earth, seeking for those whom he may destroy. If the log is going to be moved from the eye, here are two steps in the process which all must be fully aware off.

1. Avoid threatening words and actions towards others; they will escalate to more intense conflicts.

2. Do not become overly protective, since it can cause the person who thinks that he/she is in a tight spot to fight back.

Unless forgiveness is put into practice, fiery inferno will replace friendly fire; forgiveness must become a daily process. In the disciples prayer by Jesus, the word forgive is a present active participial. Forgiving is a life-long process and every individual is commanded to forgive. Some might be keeping count of sustained injustices, but forgiveness will wipe the slate clean each time it is practiced. The list might be long, but forgiveness will erase them from the God-fearing mind: *(Hebrew 10:16-17)*.

Confrontations become the inevitable when there is no forgiveness. Un-forgiveness allows ugliness to show their faces in uncontrolled rages. To those who need help through the process of forgiveness, here are a few tips:-

1. Present guilt and resentments to God and His Fiery Anointing will enable the laying down of anger and hostilities. He will take away all emotional strains from those who believe that they *"can do everything through Christ, who gives strength" (Philippians 4:13) NLT*. There is no need to doubt God's will; His promises are for the asking *(Matthew 7:7)*.

2. *"Strip off every weight that slows you down, especially the sin that so easily trips you up" (Hebrew 12:1 NLT)*. The offences will be remembered but let go the hurt.

3. Pray for offending persons. As much as possible, focus positively on them and identify something positive which can be done for them, instead of doing something spiteful, mean or unkind. At minimum, say "kind words", they will turn wrath away.

4. "Taking the log out of your own eye" is positively meeting relational tension objectively. Instead of feuding over the wrongs which others are guilty of, humbly take ownership for your contributions to the fight.

5. Take the high-road to congruity by giving another that which is rightfully yours for peace sake, it will disarm self of anger. Exonerate offenders of the mistakes which they have committed towards you. The mote that is in another person's eye can be as a speck of dust or a small grain of

sand. It is something small, but foreign to their eye. The proverbial log is large, heavy and most damning to you.

6. Moving the log is confessing faults to those who wronged you and to those whom you offended. Next, ask God for forgiveness from the urge to remove the spec from the other person's eye. When renewed minds desire these kinds of disciplines, the tongue is transformed from a weapon of mass destruction, to an instrument of blessings; it is a fire! *(James 3:6 ASV)*.

-6-

BE ON ONE ACCORD

Giving value to ideas of group members is a form of nurturing. Instead of disregarding opinions and ideas of group members, leaders should encourage unity within the group, by inviting members to share their vision for the common good of the group. Misunderstandings of visions do not discount the vision, nor does devaluing ideas of how the vision might be accomplished minimize the scope of the vision. Devaluing visions have potentials to close doors and reduce the thrust to compellingly win the fight against indifference. Exclusion of ideas from group members allow too many to become busy at tasks which can contradict the centrality of the group's vision; to be one in Christ, as He was one with the Father *(John 17:11 NASB).*

It is paradoxical at best to know that o*ne* person can be victorious against a thousand enemies and two persons can be victorious over ten thousand: *(Deuteronomy 32:30).* From this context, one can conclude that no single person will adequately bind, strangle nor eradicate conflicts. It is equally ironic when a person fights tooth and nails for an ideology that is un-proven to be better. Since selfishness violates good intended unity, it is noteworthy to remind someone that harmony is not about self-conceit, nor is it about being right. Harmony is the human-bond for valued relationship.

To appreciate friendly fire from a Scripture prospective require a centering on Biblical principles. Theological nuances differ among both members of a common group and members of the wider faith community. Community must subscribe to the rules of the game, as defined, and not to their own ideologies. Practicing God's Word, 'the Rule', will assure best results for both the group and the members of the group. Short of this, conflicts are eminent because of failure to unite in purpose; two persons cannot unite in effort unless they agree on the effort and the objective at hand: *(Amos 3:3)*.

To be grounded against conflicts is to be willing to oppose that which is contrary to the objective at hand. If oneness is going to prevail, conflicts must be squashed and kept to an absolute minimum. Here are a few fundamentals to follow, in order for division to cease:-

1. Centering Prayer.
2. *"Singleness of heart" (Ezekiel 11:19)*.
3. Shared responsibility.
4. *"Rightly dividing"* truth *(2 Timothy 2:15)*.
5. Class adaptability *(Acts 4:32)*.
6. Meet others at the point of need: *"Be it unto thee even as thou wilt" (Matthew 15:28)*.

1. Being grounded in prayer against conflicts is the believer's greatest weapon. The universal criteria common in prayer is its plea on behalf of humankind. Centering prayer requires all to pray continually. Those who have read *The Way of a Pilgrim* are familiar with the ideology of "The Jesus Prayer": *"Lord Jesus Christ, Son of God, have mercy on me, a sinner" (Luke 18:13).*

Some persons pray with accompaniments of icons or pictures, having eyes open; others were taught to pray with closed eyes, as they mystically envision Creator-God. Praying with icons is an ancient prayer practice that involves keeping the eyes wide open, and taking into the heart that which an image visually communicates. Focus is not placed on what is seen in the icon, but rather on what is seen through it - the love of God expressed through God's creation.

Icon is a form of praying without words, with a focus on being in God's presence rather than performing in God's presence. Prayer with an icon is a "right-brain" experience, touching and feeling what is mystically holy. Icons are not simply art, but a way into contemplative prayer; a way to hear God speak. They create doorways into stillness and closeness with God. Sitting long enough can transition into communion with and knowledge to obey the voice of God.

One of the four Benedictine *Lectio divina* steps is prayer. This form of prayer is usually intertwined with most forms of devotions. Prayer allows sojourners to tap into the depth and riches of *Pneuma*, be they non personal, previous or eschatological. Scripture challenge all to pray without ceasing, (Luke 18:1), in the spirit and by the commandments of God. A life of prayer minimize doubts and fears, thus facilitating a greater witness of one's faith-story.

Benedict's concept of prayerful reading, a *lectio divina* concept, is an inspiration for the inner life.[12] In prayerful reading, the contemplative soul experiences the wonders of God's handiwork and His order that gives it meaning. Benedict outlines the number of hours which should be spent at the various prayer stations. Prayerful reading, like the liturgy or manual work, is also a type of prayer. Scripture is the primary source for prayerful reading and he recommends the classics of the monastic life: the lives of the Desert Father, the *Conferences and institutes* of John Cassian, and the Rule of St. Basil.

Prayerful reading, a form of centering, is not speed reading of the Bible. It requires a technique of focus, centering on the text and an introspection of what the text is saying to the sincere and cognoscente mind. Reading the text at hand leads to a contemplative introspection of God, which will put the reader into His rest. The reader then becomes more in earnest of God's presence, His will for their life, hearing His voice and feeling His Fiery Anointing.

Usually for the Pentecostals, a non-subscriber of Benedict's *lectio divina,* prayer is verbal communications with God, alone or in concert with another. I agree with many, on the views of Russell

Spittler: "Pentecostals pray in the vernacular or in tongues, quietly or aloud, standing or kneeling, with raised arms fully overhead, palms forward, in worship and in prayer services. Although tongues can be their private prayer language, it ought to be in accordance with *"spirit" (1 Corinthians 14:15).* A second staple is *"we do not know what we ought to pray for, but the Spirit himself intercedes for us with groans that words cannot express" (Roman 8:26).*[13]

For those who might have the unction of personal glossolalia prayer, interpretation is not usually sought or expected. Praying for divine healing of the sick is commonplace in Pentecostal settings, believing that *"prayer of faith shall save the sick, and the Lord shall raise him up" (James 5:15).* Ministries of prayer on behalf of focus interests and the regular assembly of prayer groups seeking divine direction for their local group are also common. Truly, the power of prayer is a faith-walk for group members of similar persuasions, seeking to accomplish common goals.

Traditional spoken prayers display a variety of forms including invocation, novena, hymn, didactic, proclamation, exorcism, meditation, wisdom, and lamentation. They can be long like Psalm one hundred nineteen or as short as the Sumerian prayer which dates back to 2000 B.C.E. *"O God, our sins are many; strip us of them like a garment."* "Prayer may conjure or abjure, curse or jest, praise or blame, plea or giving thanks; they may be joyous, bitter, calm, choleric, charitable, or vindictive; they may burst forth at any hour, under any circumstances, in any place."[14] These variations are not unique to a particular prayer tradition, but they appeal to the needs of persons throughout the wider faith community.

Centering prayer is a popular method of contemplative prayer, placing a strong emphasis on interior silence. Centering prayer can be made with focus on a Scripture text, an idea or on something abstract. In Christian mysticism, contemplative prayer or contemplation, *theoria* (G) (θεωρία) was followed. Most often, this is not a vocal prayer or recitation of words, but a mental expressions of prayer. This recent emphasis, "centering prayer", can be traced from and through the earliest centuries of Christianity.

Centering prayer places the seeker into a right relationship with God and it is therefore mandatory for spiritual leaders, who are called to help others, to have a similar lifestyle. By so doing, spiritual leaders can better understand, through spiritual discernment, how to resist the enemy of conflict. Persons should be taught and led into forms of centering prayer, through ways which are spiritually holistic. Nothing replaces the experience of knowing God through prayer and nothing can help an individual, spirituality, better than prayer. Be them normal or specially challenged, persons are commanded to have a life of prayer. All must pray always and all must desire the spiritual gifts which come through centering prayer.

2. Maintaining singleness of group-vision demands a common spirit among all group members. The spirit of oneness in the group is not an opportunity for laity to trivialize the authority of leadership, nor is it an occasion for leadership to siphon off Sacred Ministry. As leader and laities practice how to *"be of the same mind in the Lord" (Philippians 4:2),* all will become more aware of the need to depend on Fiery Anointing. Laity will better understand that since neither they nor their leader have all the answers, both parties must seek Divine direction and wisdom, in order to overcome conflicts. Therefore, godly wisdom is paramount for unity of purpose *(Proverbs 4:7).*

The unity of a group is sufficient of itself to accomplish tasks, but only when each person in the group exercises the measure of due-diligence and faith in that vision at hand of the group. Spiritually speaking, faith is the fundamental enabler of the time and season, for the successful working of the giftedness of all participants. When beliefs that are common to the group are embraced, members will be empowered to co-exist in harmony, and resist contentions which come among them. *"Who makes you different from anyone else? What do you have that you did not receive? And if you did receive it, why do you boast as though you did not"? (1 Corinthians 4:7).*

Since most group members are oftentimes victims of perpetuated conflicts, the need to keep alive common faith practices among group members is paramount. Healthy common faith will overshadow fiery clashes amidst common group members. Common does not suggest mediocre or inferior in quality, but an equal opportunity for sharing equally in the privileges which God affords to all. Remember, humankind are created equal by God and are given equal privilege to exist in His likeness *(John 1:12 WEY)*.

God created humanities equally, with equal access and equal rights to enjoy His good pleasures. Grace is the freeway of the stratosphere by which humankind receives God's unmerited favor. Not only does grace induces desires for harmony, but grace provides all with the sustenance to continue in harmony. Fiery Anointing of God is the only giver of grace for the depraved, but humankind must respond positively to His offering in order to receive His enablement.

In order for our strength to increase through collaborative efforts, all group members - leader and laity alike - must put away the 'toys' and take up the 'tools' of Scripture. These tools allow all to resist all forms of the *"works of the flesh" (Galatians 5)*: gossip, participation in special interest groups, emotional swings, and feet that are swift to run into mischief. On the other hand, the tool is the *"fruit of the Spirit"*: sobriety, love, goodness, honesty, and truthfulness *(Galatians 5)*. The fruit of peace has always been a part of God's Divine plan for all. *"Peace I leave with you, my peace I give unto you: not as the world giveth, give I unto you. Let not your heart be troubled, neither let it be afraid" (John 14:27)*.

3. "People are an organization's most valuable asset but least used resource"[15]. Sharing of responsibilities is an investment into others, which empowers group members. Oftentimes, group members contribute more freely to organizational goals when they are invited to collaborate in friendly fires; realizing much of their self-worth through their contributions to their faith community. The laity's Call to Ministry is oftentimes highlighted through their willingness to freely give of their time and resources, as they actively buy-into and participate in the visions of their local group. To the same, leadership should continue to encourage while giving attention to all group members and affirming the Call of those who aspire to become future leaders.

Appropriate tasks should be delegated to laity who can adequately perform them. Shared leadership is supported in both the OT and NT. In the book of Exodus, Jethro advises his son-in-law, Moses, to allow others to build wholesome relationships with group members. Effective leadership was not impending by Moses's single-handed approach, so shared leadership was admonished for advancement of all concerned *(Exodus 18)*. Jesus also endorsed the principle of shared leadership, by commanding His disciples to *"follow me and I will make you fishers of men" (Matthew 4:19)*. Jesus delegated the distribution of the loaves to his disciples and they served bread to the multitude *(Matthew 14:19 NIV)*. Therefore, Biblical patterns for shared-leadership are the building-blocks for friendly fires. After all, God entrust His Fiery Anointing to those He welcomes as *"sons and daughters"*.

Shared leadership allows each group member to serve-out their passion and giftedness for Ministry. In Acts of the Apostles chapter six, the neglects by the deacons to care for the widows and the sick in the early church sparked friendly fire. This disservice motivated the Apostles to appoint additional 'help', reaffirming the Ministry of Hospitality. Expansion of their Ministerial base validates servant leadership of deacons and deaconess in faith-groups of today, propelling these groups forward.

All, but especially those who are set apart to *"prayer and the ministering of the Word", (Acts 6:3-4),* ought to continue to allow Fiery Anointing to direct and guide them away from quarrelsome administrative practices. Single handed leadership breaths contempt and conflicts breathes dishonesty. Autocracy in any form, does not give way to necessary scrutiny; instead, it invites skepticism. Jesus went to great length to avoid such conflict in leadership. *"I spake openly to the world; I ever taught in the synagogue, and in the temple, whither the Jews always resort; and in secret have I said nothing" (John 18:20).* Therefore, it is paramount that the model of shared leadership which was entrusted to the Apostles should be continued. This will allow leader and laity to build a united front against autocratic conflicts.

4. Since the Word is *truth* and it identifies the right way, governance of conflicts is a misrepresentation of the truth. *'Rightly dividing'* is the Divine standard by which intended truth of the Word is crystallized. Oftentimes, speeches and sermons that

appeal to *"itching ears" (2 Timothy 4:3)* can hardly stand-up against conflicts. The gift of persuasion is paramount and sermons and speeches ought to be embracing and appealing to those who need to turn away from conflicts. Because truth is *"foolishness to them that perish" (1 Corinthians 1:18), truth* ought never to be camouflaged. Cordial and convincing sermons and speeches must give needed assurance that harmony is a better way.

5. Encouraging class adaptability is akin to *"having all things common" (Acts 4:32).* Those who are members of multi-cultured groups, should be encouraged to strive to always exercise cohesive fellowship, and desire to shun disruptive conflicts. A group member should never be told by a group leader that their participation is not welcomed, because the leader is not educated about cultural differences of the member. Instead, deliberate attempts must be taken by leaders of the group, to break-down dividing walls which ostracized member. Plural leadership will safeguard against communal implosion of this type.

Like nepotism, conflicts through spiritual apathy undermine a group of its strength. All forms of exclusion and favoritism against members in a group must cease from depriving group members of harmony; intentional divides suggest 'spiritual darkness'. Harmony is singular and its terms and agreement are singular unto God. Any force to eradicate conflicts must also be singular in purpose, since He who demands unity is singular. *"By one Spirit are we all baptized into one body" (1 Corinthians 12:13).*

When Jesus cried from the cross *"it is finished"*, *(John 19:30)*, His voice ricocheted from the walls of the temple, and reverberating power of these three words split the veil which divided the temple into two separate pieces. Those present became immediately aware that the *"Holy of Holy"* was accessible to all, through Jesus' redemptive work on the cross. The echo of His cry bound together classes of temple worshipers one last time, liberating them from indifferences, making them one people unto God.

6. Meeting others at their point of need is an act of caring for another. Scripture declares, *"Be it unto thee even as thou wilt" (Matthew 15:28)*. By so doing, a group member will be facilitated to affirm an idea of another member. Ideas are either timely or premature for the moment and spending time putting forward an untimely idea might generally be seen as unconstructive. Time invested into maintaining the bond of peace is never wasted *(1Corinthians 3:7)*.

Reaching-out to others should never be seen as a proverbial target practice, nor as something to establish prominence among group members. Throwing content out and watching to see what happens next is a form of target practice. Telling about and witnessing the transforming power of God, should always be the objective of the messenger who dwells and serves in the spirit of harmony. All faith group members must take part in regular study of God's word, so that they would be quickened by His self-same spirit, in order that they might meet others at their point of need.

Remember when Jesus was challenged by the Syrophoenician woman to help her daughter? The will of God for this woman did not allow *"The Son of Man"* to continue with His Judaic theology: *"I was sent only to the lost sheep of the house of Israel" (Matthew 15:24).* Since the wishes of the woman were in conflict with Jesus' mission at that time, His disciples wanted Him to send her away. It was the faith of this woman that daunted Jesus to back-off from what He was about and meet her at her point of need.

The practical theology of this woman, who wanted her demon-possessed daughter to enjoy freedom from her conflicts, challenged Jesus. Jesus likening the woman to a dog became the single greatest moment of her life; for she understood that this lowly dog-like status could not deprived her of *the crumbs.* Although *crumbs* were the bare minimal which a dog enjoys, her lowly classification gave birth to the greatest faith that a no-named woman could enjoy. Jesus was compelled by the woman's faith, so he healed her daughter. Until there is a turning away from self-center-ness to showing care one for each other, harmony will be theoretical at best.

-7-
GLORIFY GOD FROM THE FIRE.

Humankind is made both in the image of God and for the glory of God, so these privileges make glorifying Him foundational. In good times, exalting Him is often overlooked because humankind is a glory-seeking being. When engulfed by life's infernos and fighting for relief is also brought-on. Times of conflicts are not times for complaining and festering against those who did wrong. Instead of becoming testy, defensive or confrontational when conflicts show up, glorify He who quenches every fiery dart of the enemy.

Kabod (H), and *doxa (G),* translate *glory*[16], and support the translation of glory as "genuineness". Both root words summarize the worthiness, perfection and infinite significance of God. *Kabod and doxa* sums up the awesomeness of God's majesty. God is totally magnificent and loving, and He beckons continuously to the fallen and depraved to turn away from meaningless contentions. He commands that everything be done for His glory: *(1 Corinthians 10:31).*

Like the "three Hebrew boys" of the Old Testament, Paul and Silas are two of the poster-boys of the New Testament who glorified God from their fiery trials. They were placed in prison for preaching the Gospel and their prayers for freedom were answered at midnight by God, through one of His miraculous earthquake. A jailor on duty met-up with a conflict of unfaithfulness to his watch, thinking that Paul and Silas escaped from his protective custody. In fear of being tortured to death for allowing this dishonorable act, the jailor attempted to fast forward his would-be punishment. Without a doubt, God was glorified when Paul and Silas rescued the jailor from suicide.

Imagine the rescue of this villain, the jailor who participated in the cruel punishment of Paul and Silas. The jailor was loyal to his commander, but he knew that the punishment was cruel and unjust. Although the jailor made himself an enemy to his captives, yet still Paul and Silas engaged him in friendly fire. God's divine favor prevailed when it was Paul and Silas turn to get even with the jailor's losses, but instead, they glorified God by entreating him: *"not to harm himself!" (Acts 16:28 NASB).* Believers ought to be equally compassionate to those who desire harm upon them. God blesses those who are persecuted for righteousness sake: *(Matthew 5:11).*

See conflicts as opportunities for friendly fire and not times to take revenge. Reflecting on God's wisdom, power, and love will convince all who desire to praise Him when their world seems to be on fire. Godly wisdom brings about the peace of God in the hearts and minds of individuals and Fiery Anointing provides the faith needed to rise above every negative influence of the enemy. This Anointing can propel all to do "good" to those who despitefully use them and allows a *"springing up" (John 4:14)* of empathy in their hearts, so that they would *"resist" (James 4:7)* the urges to become score-keepers against their attackers.

Glorifying God amidst frustrations and tensions can allow the wounded to rise above repulsion and shame which conflicts bring. Praises and thanksgiving unto God will lift their spirit above the shadows of discouragements. When they are distracted from peaceable times, God's grace and mercies can stop them from falling downward any further. If by chance that they do fall, He can cushion their plunge, thus inducing His unmerited favor to reach down and pick them up. Be thankful and bless God's name for His everlasting mercy and His loving kindness are better than life: *"O give thanks unto the LORD, for he is good: for his mercy endureth forever" (Psalm 107).*

In the heat of the battle, the challenge is, too often, to defend self. Instead, shift focus away from self, in order that God's glory might be seen. Jesus faced His hottest conflict after He was arrested; suffering cruel mocking, persecutions, denial, beatings (forty stripes – less one), crucifixion, then death on a rugged cross. Amidst them all, His testimony lives on: He who was sinless died for the sins of the world: *(Philippians 2:8-11).*

As the humility of the cross is relived, walking in the steps of Jesus is equally possible. All must glorify God as Jesus did on the cross; making humility their single greatest state of mind. Jesus could have called ten-thousand angels to launch an all-out attack against

His enemies, but He was meek and mild. Meekness is still the maxim for reconciliation. Meekness will put believers in mind to submit to the Spirit of God and local authority, be compassionate and be humble before God: *(Titus 3: 1-2)*. So remain meek and humble in the heat of every battle and stand still as the deliverance of the Lord is enjoyed. Open the eyes and see the manifestation of His glory!

The word of God became flesh and came to mother earth in His glory and majesty. Through the telescope of time, the Prophet Isaiah saw *"the whole earth fill with his glory" (Isaiah 6:3)*. This glory announces His Omnipotence, Omnipresence, Omniscience and His Omni-benevolence; He is to be accredited with the eminence due to His name through praises and adorations. Give Him glory for his protection from the heat of conflicts; He will honor all sincere efforts of praises unto Him and transend blessings to all who desires them.

In the name of peace, declare His distinction among friend and foe, and invite others to join in with expressions of praise for God's delightful presence. Join His creation as they glorify Him: trees are clapping, winds are hauling, seas are roaring, birds are singing and thunders are rolling. Therefore, there is no reason for those who were made a little lower than angels not to give God glory. So let us all shout praises to His wonderful name and watch the transformation of conflicts into showers of blessings!

> *"O LORD, our Lord,*
> *how majestic is your name in all the earth!*
> *You have set your glory above the heavens.*
> *From the lips of children and infants*
> *you have ordained praise because of your enemies,*
> *to silence the foe and the avenger.*
> *When I consider your heavens,*
> *the work of your fingers, the moon and the stars,*
> *which you have set in place,*
> *what is man that you are mindful of him,*
> *the son of man that you care for him?*
> *(Psalm 8:1-4 NIV).*

Reconciliation glorifies God and it is primary to any gift which can be offered to Him *(Matthew 5:23-24).* Biblical methods to peacemaking invoke commitment to forgiveness and help to restore damaged relationships. The heart might be pounding because of words of slander or maybe because of a physical confrontation of a kind or another. Eyes might be teary, tongue might be stammering and spoken words slurred because of emotional hurts. Blame by others might be more than that which one desires to bear. The rational mind may have decreed that the villain should not escape punishment for the wrong which was done. Whatever is the situation, glorifying God gives best leverage.

Eugene Peterson writes, "So don't be embarrassed to speak up for our Master or for me, his prisoner. Take your share of suffering for the Message along with the rest of us. We can only keep on going, after all, by the power of God, who first saved us and then called us to this holy work. We had nothing to do with it. It was all his idea, a gift prepared for us in Jesus long before we knew anything about it. But we know it now. Since the appearance of our Savior, nothing could be plainer: death defeated, life vindicated in a steady blaze of light, all through the work of Jesus".[17] Reconciliation enables cooperative negotiation which seeks agreements that are just and satisfactory to others, in spite of who said, who did or who did not.

Best practice for reconciliation with believers is reaffirmed in the Gospel of Matthew chapter eighteen. Offences will come but they should be kept to a minimum (v7). When a person is offended by another, the victim should *"go and tell* (the villain) *his fault between you and him alone" (Matthew 18:15 AKJV).* As was required under the law, the offended person was commanded to: *"Go and reprove him" (Leviticus 19:17)* to himself. Mitigating the offence often require friendly fire between both parties, especially when the information which is causing the offence is second-handed. Friendly and brotherly reproof should be given to the plaintiff for similar reasons below:

1. The plaintiff would have an opportunity to clarify their conduct. Whenever one is offended, a little friendly fire can set the matter right.

2. If, in fact wrong was caused to another, the plaintiff would have an opportunity to acknowledge his offence and make necessary reparation for the offence; stay close to the accuser.

3. Admonish the offender, hater or the erred person; if an injury has been made to the cause of wholesome relationships. It will do little good, causing a greater degree of pain, if the fault was blazoned about. Remember, the purpose of the enemy is to cause pain. The wounded will suffer additional pains and Christ will be crucified afresh, if the fault is blazon about.

Scripture commands that brethren must be keeper of each other, making them equally responsible for the other's wellbeing. When wild-fires occur, the plaintiff and the defendant must seek to put the fire out swiftly and in unison, before involving mediators. Disobeying this guideline of Scripture in any form makes the defendant equally at fault as the perpetrator of the conflict. So then, at what point in the conflict should mediators be brought into the reconciliation process? How would either the plaintiff or the defendant know the right time to invite another?

Brotherly love must triumph at all cost among group members: *"if he listens to you, you have won your brother over" (15b NIV).* To win means, to preserve, to save or to gain, as noted in First Corinthians chapter nine and verse nineteen: *"For though I am free from all men, I have made myself a slave to all, so that I may win more".* Winning in this context is restoring a broken relationship to caring one-to and one-for another. This process would generally have all the desired benefits of reconciling the plaintiff and the defendant, and this principle, which is too often neglected, should be practiced under all circumstances. Although not enough group members attempt this method which Christ enjoins, living peaceably with each other requires ongoing reconciliation.

Glorifying God demands that group members put away their indifferences and desire to co-exist in harmony. For too long, members of common faith group have adopted the carnal views of the world: *"my way or the highway"*. Too often, members become estranged from their place of spiritual nurturing because they cannot have that which they, selfishly, deem necessary to them. Too often, members are unwilling to compromise in the name of spiritual unity and singleness of heart; suggesting that they do not understand Matthew eighteen, verse fifteen, will no longer be acceptable. Winning offenders remain the responsibility of all accusers and loving others as self remains the second greatest commandment, to that of loving God wholly. The thought of "when we all get to Heaven" is wasted without reconciliation one-to-another!

Conflicts steal the joy of their victims, but Scripture affirms persistence in reconciliation. *"If (*the villain) *will not hear thee, then take with thee one or two more, that in the mouth of two or three witnesses every word may be established" (v16).* Failure to make a breakthrough with the erred party is the clue that conciliatory help is needed. Since the natural mind will hardly guide an accuser through friendly fire with a defendant, spiritual perception and discernment are best dependencies. Usually, a friend or a family member is the first reference as conciliator, but this approach is only good if the conciliator can remain impartial. Preconceived notions by friends and family can bias negotiations, so choose mediators who can be most authentic to the process of amicable resolutions.

Applying the methods of verses fifteen and sixteen above can become unsuccessful for various reasons. As the complainant, do not wait for the wrongdoer to start the process, but make the first step by going to the defendant. It is OK to accept a loss of that which was wronged, if the desire is not to have the faith group to resolve the issue at hand. To this decision, there remains a compelling option to cover the offense in love. *"Stay wide-awake in prayer."*[18] *(1 Peter 4:7-9 AB)*.

Scripture advises in favors of public resolution of conflicts, as an accelerated solution: *"If he shall neglect to hear them, tell it to the church" (Matthew 18:17)*. Group members are not given lee-way to resolve conflicts through the judicial system. Church in this context suggests official meetings by the faith group, and since the business is for the local group, resolving conflicts publically by the local leaders are for the benefit of the membership. The House of Prayer is the public forum where The Gifts of the Spirit dwell for smooth, peaceable and palatable resolution of all conflicts: *saints will judge the world: (1 Corinthians 6:2)!*

Conflicts, schism and hypocrisy stir-up divisive confusions. Division brings unhappiness which subsequently brings death. God's word says peace and safety but the adversary says obliteration and ruin. Unity is strength, not an instrument of strength. From the beginning of time, the Determinate Counsel demonstrated that the Father, Son, and Holy Ghost are united; therefore, peace is present when group members are united in purpose, action and efforts of glorifying God from the fire. Conciliation must be an opportunity to resolve differences and disputes and the process is to be peace-making rather than adversarial. Conciliators are to encourage honest communication and reasonable cooperation, rather than confrontational escalation of contention and advocacy.

Glorifying God through conflict reconciliation will define another aspect of the witness and worship of His people, making His authority visible throughout their lives and ministries. Worship is not just attending meetings on high-days, but more importantly a commitment to worshipping continually. Not only did the angel who appeared to the shepherds worshipped as he announced the coming of the glory of God, but this Heavenly splendor soon gave way to a crescendo of glorifying God by *"a multitude of the heavenly host" (Luke 2:13).* They worshipped the Son of God as the wise men appreciated Him with their gifts.

Humankind who is made a little lower than angels can hardly imagine the glory, majesty and brightness of angels. Just as *"an angel of the Lord" (Luke 2:9)* did, a single person can glorify God, be it from the fire or otherwise, victim or villain. In times of tension, conflicts and confusions, praises can press tense moments into oblivious and defeats. So at the next moment of frustration, shout *Hosanna (G)*! Save me, I pray!

Instead of focusing on the setbacks which conflicts bring, remember the promises that the tables of delights are spread *"in the presence of enemies" (Psalm 23:5).* Recalling unpleasant attitudes or negative behaviors by perpetrators might be commonplace, but the peace of Christ will continue to fill hearts of those who are wrestling with offences. He shows forth His favor to those who invite Him to be their conciliator. Those who might find themselves in the despair of conflicts can always ask Him to give them the spirit of grace and glory.

Like the many who relied on Fiery Anointing, both in Biblical and post Biblical times, to overcome conflicts, Stephen glorified God by praying for the forgiveness of some who *"disput*ed*" (Acts 6:9)* against him. Perhaps Paul and Silas were able to obtain the best attorney and could have received bale, but they glorified God from their prison. Prayer-waives shook the earth where the prison stood, rattling locked doors to swing open and shackles to fall from their hands and ankles: *(Acts 16:26).* Prayer rocks!

No longer should relationships be trivialized by sinister behaviors. No longer should individuals engage in tit-for-tat conducts, but they should allow camaraderie to guide them from conflicts. Times of fellowship will become spontaneous, when forgiveness and praises take residence in hearts.

Those having renewed minds and worshipping God in the spirit, *(Philippians 3:3),* take lead! Ignore the things of the flesh and glorify God in the midst of conflicts. Flesh includes anything which is not spiritual or anything sensual; an evil thought, speaking that which can offend another or willfully doing that which brings offense to another. What a wonderful day that would be when all would be declared noble!

Freedom of giving worship, praises and glory to God must become the supreme passion and vocation of all. As each exhale fills the earth with majesty, conflicts will be silenced; God wants every tongue, every tribe and every nation to declare His glory in all the earth: (*1 Chronicles 16:24*). He demands glory*: "I will not give my glory unto another" (Isaiah 48:11).*

Therefore, Let God's glory rise, pressing the rage of conflicts into cessation and famine. Let the praises of the King of glory rise in the office places, in homes, through good times of plenty and through times of famine. Let hosanna rise to the King above, in the midst of weariness and heavy of heart. Let glory rise above the gossipers, circling those who repeat that which they should not have heard. Let the glory of God fill the whole earth, so that social ills would lose their sting and retreat their assassination of the integrity of the innocent. Let the joys of knowing that the Lord of peace trumps every conflict. O……h, Oh, O…..h. Let His glory rise[19]!

CONCLUSION

No longer should there be doubts about the Divine nature of Christ. No longer should there be uncertainty of His miracles and His offer of eternal deliverance through grace; He is Savior of the world Matthew (1:21). Whatever the questions might be, all must continue to push through their faith-struggles in Christ. At one point, Paul too, had conflicts with the authority of Jesus, but his testimony in one of his Epistles is his witness that he was not ashamed of the gospel of Christ: *(Romans 1:16).*

God is awesome! And His Lordship makes Him healer, deliverer, way-maker, comforter and ruler. He is all powerful, making him Omnipotent: *"All power is given to me both in heaven and in earth" (Matthew 28:18).* Through this power, He will deliver all from every form of conflicts. His Omnipresence places Him everywhere at the same time and His presence everywhere simultaneously gives him authority over His entire creation: *"the heaven and heaven of heavens cannot contain thee"? (1 Kings 8:27).* Omnipresence is more than attributes, since attributes can be considered as add-ons; therefore, efforts to describe God is floored.

God's immeasurable compassion makes Him Omni-benevolent. Again, Paul reminds all that God expresses His love for all through Christ's death on the cross (Romans 5:8), as humankind is sinful. It is wonderful to know that He *"gave his only begotten son (John*

3:16) for the redemption of all; oh how he loves you and me! No one can change the mind of God towards his creation.

Through His infinite knowing, he is Omniscient *(2 Chronicles 16:9)*. He knows all things at all times and He can never be tricked, misled, manipulated or dictated to. He is wider than all the oceans when concatenated, higher than all the mountains stacked all on each other and deeper than all the valleys when hanging together. Humankind both knows in part because knowledge is revealed to each one in part; but when completeness comes, the finite is transformed into infinite. God's inestimable knowledge trumps conflicts!

One of the many lessons Jesus taught in "the Sermon on the Mount" is forgiveness: *(Matthew 6:14-15)*. Forgiveness is a work of salvation, a word mentioned 143 times in the New Testament. Forgiveness is letting-go of grudges, resentment, ill-will, bitterness or the chip on the shoulder. It is releasing another from obligation or choosing to cancel something which another owes. Forgiveness allows fire with all accusers to be friendly.

Forgiveness of conflict culprits is both a crises and a process. Defending oneself is a normal process especially when a person behaves violently or acts unjustly. The process continues through living-out the hurt and letting go of the pain over time. Jewish law says three-times then out and Peter thought that he was a good fellow by forgiving his accusers seven times. Perhaps, he thought that if he doubled the number of times from three to six, plus one, Jesus would have given him brownie-points. Perhaps he was expecting Jesus to say 'you are a great guy', 'you are a very considerate person'.

How soon did Peter forget that the ways of God are not the ways of men? Instead, Jesus told him that he should forgive his accusers seventy times seven in one day. This does not mean seven plus sever nor does it means seventy plus seven times; but *"490 times in one day" (Matthew 18:22).* In other words, do not count the number of times you forgave a person for creating conflicts. Since true forgiveness has no limits, he who fails in the process, will live in the crises.

Conflict resolution is a reachable goal and the choice is to forgive *(Matthew 6:14),* rather than withholding grudges. Do not be a score keeper, but instead, let go of anything which will hinder you from showing genuine love to others. See the best in others.

Appendices

Scripture References

Warming Up

P13: *"Why do the nations rage and the peoples meditate a vain thing?" (Psalm 2:1 ASV).*

P14: *but "God will provide a way out so that (All) can stand up under it" (1 Corinthians 10:13 NIV)*

P15: *"Love your neighbor as yourself" (Leviticus 19:18)*

Chapter One

P18: "out of the iron-smelting furnace, out of Egypt, to be the people of God's inheritance" (Deuteronomy 4:20). Because

P19: "When thou walkest through the fire, thou shalt not be burned" (Isaiah 43:2).

P19: "I will go over and see this strange sight-why the bush does not burn up" (Exodus 3:3).

P20: "The branch cannot bear fruit of itself, except it abide in the vine" (John 15:4) .

P20: "That there should be no schism in the body; but that the members should have the same care one for another" (1 Corinthians 15:25)

P20: "The acts of the sinful nature are obvious: sexual immorality, impurity and debauchery; idolatry and witchcraft; hatred, discord, jealousy, fits of rage, selfish ambition, dissensions, factions and envy; drunkenness, orgies, and the like" (Galatians 5:19-21 NIV).

P21: "Every child of God defeats this evil world through faith" (1 John 5:4 NLT)

P21: "All of you agree with one another so that there may be no divisions among you and that you may be perfectly united in mind and thought" group (1 Corinthians 1:10 NIV).

P23: When we are slandered, we answer kindly. Up to this moment we have become the scum of the earth, the refuse of the world" (1 Corinthians 4:13 NIV).

Chapter Two

P74: *"Holy Father, keep them in Your name, the name which You have given Me, that they may be one even as We are" (John 17:11 NASB).*

P74: *"How should one chase a thousand, and two put ten thousand to flight, except their Rock had sold them, and the LORD had given them up?"* (Deuteronomy 32:30).

P75: *"Can two walk together, except they be agreed?" (Amos 3:3).*

P75: *"And I will give them one heart, and I will put a new spirit within you; and I will take the stony heart out of their flesh, and will give them an heart of flesh" (Ezekiel 11:19).*

P75: *"Study to shew thyself approved unto God, a workman that needeth not to be ashamed, rightly dividing the word of truth" (2 Timothy 2:15).*

P75: *"And the multitude of them that believed were of one heart and of one soul: neither said any of them that ought of the things which he possessed was his own; but they had all things common" (Acts 4:32)*

P75: *"Jesus answered and said unto her, O woman, great is thy faith: be it unto thee even as thou wilt. And her daughter was made whole from that very hour" (Matthew 15:28).*

P76: *"Lord Jesus Christ, Son of God, have mercy on me, a sinner" (Luke 18:13).*

P78: *"spirit" (1 Corinthians 14:15)*

P78: "the prayer of faith shall save the sick, and the Lord shall raise him up; and if he have committed sins, they shall be forgiven him" (James 5:15).

P80: "I plead with Euodia and I plead with Syntyche to be of the same mind in the Lord" (Philippians 4:2).

P80: "Wisdom is the principal thing; therefore get wisdom: and with all thy getting get understanding" (Proverbs 4:7).

P80: "Who makes you different from anyone else? What do you have that you did not receive? And if you did receive it, why do you boast as though you did not"? (1 Corinthians 4:7).

P81: "But all who have received Him, to them-that is, to those who trust in His name-He has given the privilege of becoming children of God" lege to exist in His likeness (John 1:12 WEY)

P81: "But the fruit of the Spirit is love, joy, peace, patience..." (Galatians 5:22-23).

P81: "Peace I leave with you, my peace I give unto you: not as the world giveth, give I unto you. Let not your heart be troubled, neither let it be afraid" (John 14:27)

P82: " provide out of all the people able men, such as fear God, men of truth, hating covetousness; and place such over them, to be rulers of thousands, and rulers of hundreds, rulers of fifties, and rulers of tens: And let them judge the people at all seasons: and it shall be, that every great matter they shall bring unto thee, but every small matter they shall judge: so shall it be easier for thyself, and they shall bear the burden with thee." (Exodus 18:21-22 NIV)

P82: "Follow me, and I will make you fishers of men" (Matthew 4:19)

P82: "Then he gave them to the disciples, and the disciples gave them to the people" (Matthew 14:19 NIV).

P83: "look ye out among you seven men of honest report, full of the Holy Ghost and wisdom, whom we may appoint over this business. But we will give ourselves continually to prayer, and to the ministry of the word" (Acts 6:3-4)

P83: "I spake openly to the world; I ever taught in the synagogue, and in the temple, whither the Jews always resort; and in secret have I said nothing" (John 18:20)

P84: "By one Spirit are we all baptized into one body, whether we be Jews or Gentiles, whether we be bond or free; and have been all made to drink into one Spirit" (1 Corinthians 12:13).

P85: "When Jesus therefore had received the vinegar, he said, It is finished: and he bowed his head, and gave up the ghost" (John 19:30).

P85: "I therefore, the prisoner of the Lord, beseech you that ye walk worthy of the vocation wherewith ye are called, With all lowliness and meekness, with longsuffering, forbearing one another in love; Endeavoring to keep the unity of the Spirit in the bond of peace." bond of peace is never wasted (1Corinthians 3:7).

P86: "I was sent only to the lost sheep of the house of Israel" (Matthew 15:24).

Chapter Three

P24: "the people that walked in darkness have seen a great light: they that dwell in the land of the shadow of death, upon them hath the light shined" (Isaiah 9:2).

P25: "And God said, "let there be light" (Genesis 1:3)

P25: "But when the fullness of the time was come, God sent forth his Son, made of a woman, made under the law, To redeem them that were under the law, that we might receive the adoption of sons" (Galatians 4:4-5).

P27: "The sun is the light to rule the day and the moon and the stars to rule the night" (Psalm 136:8-9).

P27: "Watch over your heart with all diligence, for from it flow the springs of life" (Proverbs 4:23 NASB).

P28: "Ye are the light of the world. A city that is set on an hill cannot be hid" (Matthew 5:14).

P28: "No one can serve two masters. For you will hate one and love the other; you will be devoted to one and despise the other." (Luke 16:13 NLT).

P28: "Now we see through a glass, darkly; but then face to face: now I know in part; but then shall I know even as also I am known" (1 Corinthians 13:12).

P30" "Declare ye in Judah, and publish in Jerusalem; and say, Blow ye the trumpet in the land: cry, gather together, and say, Assemble yourselves, and let us go into the defenced cities" (Jeremiah 4:5)

P30: "After my departing shall grievous wolves enter in among you, not sparing the flock. Also of your own selves shall men arise, speaking perverse things, to draw away disciples after them" (Acts 20:29).

P30: "And he saith unto them, Follow me, and I will make you fishers of men" (Matthew 4:19).

P31: "I am he that liveth, and was dead; and, behold, I am alive for evermore, Amen; and have the keys of hell and of death" (Revelation 1:18).

P31: "I have told you these things so that in Me you may have peace. You will have suffering in this world. Be courageous! I have conquered the world" (John 16:33 HCSB).

P31: "The people that walked in darkness have seen a great light: they that dwell in the land of the shadow of death, upon them hath the light shined" (Isaiah 9:2)

P32: "You are not far from the kingdom of God." "Which commandment is the most important of them all" (Mark 12:30 ISV)

P32: "A soft answer turneth away wrath: grievous words stir up anger" (Proverbs 15:1).

P32: "But he, willing to justify himself, said unto Jesus, And who is my neighbour?" (Luke 10:29 NIV).

P33: "These twelve Jesus sent out, charging them, "Go nowhere among the Gentiles, and enter no town of the Samaritans, but go rather to the lost sheep of the house of Israel" (Matthew 10:5 ESV).

P33: "Ye have heard that it hath been said, Thou shalt love thy neighbour, and hate thine enemy. But I say unto you, Love your enemies, bless them that curse you, do good to them that hate you, and pray for them which despitefully use you, and persecute you" (Matthew 5:43-44).

P33: "Honour thy father and thy mother: and, Thou shalt love thy neighbour as thyself" (Matthew 19:19).

P35: "For by him were all things created, that are in heaven, and that are in earth, visible and invisible, whether they be thrones, or dominions, or principalities, or powers: all things were created by him, and for him: And he is before all things, and by him all things consist. And he is the head of the body, the church: who is the beginning, the firstborn from the dead; that in all things he might have the preeminence" (Colossians 1:16-18).

Chapter Four

P37: "The LORD said, "What have you done? Listen! Your brother's blood cries out to me from the ground" (Genesis 4:10).

P38: "Where is Abel your brother?" He said, "I do not know" (Genesis 4:9 NAS).

P39: "I find then a law, that, when I would do good, evil is present with me" (Romans 7:21).

P39: "All that is in the world, the lust of the flesh, and the lust of the eyes, and the pride of life, is not of the Father, but is of the world" (1 John 2:16).

P39: "There is therefore now no condemnation to them which are in Christ Jesus" (Galatians 6:8).

P40: "Now is come salvation, and strength, and the kingdom of our God, and the power of his Christ: for the accuser of our brethren is cast down which accused them from our God day and night. (Revelation 12:10 NLT)

P40: "And Jesus knew their thoughts, and said unto them, Every kingdom divided against itself is brought to desolation; and every city or house divided against itself shall not stand" (Matthew 12:25).

P40: "Cast out the scorner, and contention shall go out; yea, strife and reproach shall cease" with it, (Proverb 22:10).

P40: "God is not a God of confusion, but of peace. As in all the churches of the saints" (1 Corinthians 14:33).

P41: "Disgrace is before ruin and pride of spirit before misfortune" (Proverbs 16:18 AR).

P41: "I appeal to you, brothers, in the name of our Lord Jesus Christ, that all of you agree with one another so that there may be no divisions among you and that you may be perfectly united in mind and thought" (1 Corinthians 1:10 NIV).

P41: "For the kingdom of heaven is like a landowner who went out early in the morning to hire workers for his vineyard. He agreed to pay them a denarius[a] for the day and sent them into his vineyard" (Matthew 20:2)

P42: "Abram said to Lot, I pray thee let there be no contention between me and thee, and between my herdsmen and thy herdsmen, for we are brethren. (Genesis 13:8 DBT).

P43: "What is causing the quarrels and fights among you? Don't they come from the evil desires at war within you? You want what you don't have, so you scheme and kill to get it. You are jealous of what others have, but you can't get it, so you fight and wage war to take it away from them. Yet you don't have what you want because you don't ask God for it" (James 4:1-2 NLT)

P43: "The acts of the flesh are obvious: sexual immorality, impurity and debauchery; idolatry and witchcraft; hatred, discord, jealousy, fits of rage, selfish ambition, dissensions, factions and envy; drunkenness, orgies, and the like" Galatians 5:19-21) NIV

P43: "For ye are yet carnal: for whereas there is among you envying, and strife, and divisions, are ye not carnal, and walk as men"? grows envious, then separated from spiritual harmony (1 Corinthians 3:3).

P44: *"Don't just pretend to love others. Really love them. Hate what is wrong. Hold tightly to what is good"* (Romans 12:9 NLT).

P44: *"And ought not this woman, being a daughter of Abraham, whom Satan hath bound, lo, these eighteen years, be loosed from this bond on the sabbath day?"* on the Sabbath day.

P45: *"A thief does not come except to steal, kill and destroy; I have come that they may have life and have whatever is abundant"* (John 10:10 MASB)

P45: *"The enemy hath persecuted my soul; he hath smitten my life down to the ground; he hath made me to dwell in darkness, as those that have been long dead"* (Psalm 143:3)

P45: *"stand against the wiles of the enemy"* (Ephesians 6:11).

P46: And all that believed were together, and had all things common" (Acts 2:44

P46: *"I do not do the good I want, but the evil I do not want is what I keep on doing"* (Romans 7:19 ESV).

P47: *"Restore such an one in the spirit of meekness; considering thyself, lest thou also be tempted. Bear ye one another's burdens, and so fulfill the law of Christ"* (Galatians 6:1-2).

P47: *"Let your speech be always with grace, seasoned with salt, that ye may know how ye ought to answer every man"* (Colossians 4:6).

P48: "The beginning of strife is as when one letteth out water: therefore leave off contention, before it be meddled with" (Proverb 17:14).

P48: "But avoid foolish questions, and genealogies, and contentions, and strivings about the law; for they are unprofitable and vain" (Titus 3:9).

P49: "Dare any of you, having a matter against another, go to law before the unjust, and not before the saints? (1 Corinthians 6:1-3).

Chapter Five

P50: *"For we wrestle not against flesh and blood, but against principalities" (Ephesians 6:11)*

P55: *"My people are destroyed for lack of knowledge: because thou hast rejected knowledge"* for those who lack knowledge *(Hosea 4:6).*

P55 *"Resist the devil, and he will flee from you" (James 4:7).*

P56: *"Fear thou not; for I am with thee: be not dismayed; for I am thy God: I will strengthen thee; yea, I will help thee; yea, I will uphold thee with the right hand of my righteousness" (Isaiah 41:10).*

P56: *"Jesus said unto him, I am the way, the truth, and the life: no man comes unto the Father, but by me" (John 14:6)*

P56: *"Jesus Christ the same yesterday, and today, and forever" (Hebrews 13:8).*

P56: *"These things I have spoken unto you, that in me ye might have peace. In the world ye shall have tribulation: but be of good cheer; I have overcome the world" (John 16:33).*

P56: *"And they shall scourge him, and put him to death: and the third day he shall rise again" (Luke 18:13).*

P56: *"If I go and prepare a place for you, I will come again, and receive you unto myself; that where I am, there ye may be also" (John 14:3).*

P57: *"Unto us a child is born, unto us a son is given: and the government shall be upon his shoulder: and his name shall* be called Wonderful, Counseller, The mighty God, The everlasting Father, The Prince of Peace" (Isaiah 9:6).

P57: "What shall we then say to these things? If God be for us, who can be against us?" (Romans 8:31).

P58: "The LORD shall make thee the head, and not the tail; and thou shalt be above only, and thou shalt not be beneath; if that thou hearken unto the commandments of the LORD thy God, which I command thee this day, to observe and to do them" (Deuteronomy 28:13).

P58: "a sinner's wealth is stored up for the righteous" (Proverbs 13:22).

P59: "But ye are a chosen generation, a royal priesthood, an holy nation, a peculiar people; that ye should shew forth the praises of him who hath called you out of darkness into his marvellous light" (1 Peter 2:9).

P59: "And in that day ye shall ask me nothing. Verily, verily, I say unto you, Whatsoever ye shall ask the Father in my name, he will give it you" (John 16:23)

P59: "Wherefore putting away lying, speak every man truth with his neighbour: for we are members one of another" (Ephesians 5:25).

P59: "No weapon that is formed against thee shall prosper; and every tongue that shall rise against thee in judgment thou shalt condemn. This is the heritage of the servants of the LORD, and their righteousness is of me, saith the LORD" (Isaiah 54:17).

P59: "Fear ye not, stand still, and see the salvation of the LORD, which he will show to you today: for the Egyptians *whom ye have seen today, ye shall see them again no more forever" (Exodus 14:13).*

P60: *Who may dwell in your sanctuary? Who may live on your holy hill? He whose walk is blameless and who does what is righteous, who speaks the truth from his heart and has no slander on his tongue, who does his neighbor no wrong and casts no slur on his fellowman, who despises a vile man but honors those who fear the LORD, who keeps his oath even when it hurts, who lends his money without usury and does not accept a bribe against the innocent. He who does these things will never be shaken. (Psalm 15 NIV).*

P60: *"Be not deceived; God is not mocked: for whatsoever a man soweth, that shall he also reap" (Galatians 6:7).*

P61: *"A heart that devises wicked imaginations, feet that are swift in running to evil" (Proverbs 6:18).*

P62: *"Whosoever shall say unto this mountain, Be thou removed, and be thou cast into the sea; and shall not doubt in his heart, but shall believe that those things which he saith shall come to pass; he shall have whatsoever he saith" (Mark 11:23).*

P63: *"For the word of God is quick, and powerful, and sharper than any twoedged sword, piercing even to the dividing asunder of soul and spirit, and of the joints and marrow, and is a discerner of the thoughts and intents of the heart" (Hebrews 4:12).*

P64: "O God, thou art my God; early will I seek thee: my soul thirsteth for thee, my flesh longeth for thee in a dry and thirsty land, where no water is" *(Psalm 63:1-2).*

P64: "Lest Satan should get an advantage of us: for we are not ignorant of his devices" *(2 Corinthians 2:11)*

P65: "Since the days of John the Baptist until now the kingdom of heaven suffereth violence, and the violent take it by force" *(Matthew 11:12).*

Chapter Six

P66: *"Therefore, rid yourselves of every kind of evil and deception, hypocrisy, jealousy, and every kind of slander"* to get rid of hypocrisy *(1Peter 2:1 ISV).*

P66: *"Hypocrite! First get rid of the log in your own eye; then you will see well enough to deal with the speck in your friend's eye" (Matthew 7:5 NLT).*

P67: *"Judge not, that ye be not judged. For with what judgment ye judge, ye shall be judged: and with what measure ye mete, it shall be measured to you again" (Matthew 7:1-2).*

P68: *"If a man be overtaken in a fault, ye which are spiritual, restore such an one in the spirit of meekness" (Galatians 6:1).*

P69: *"not to pay anyone back evil for evil, but focus* [their] *thoughts on what is right in the sight of all people" (Romans 12:17 ISV).*

P69: *"I am giving you my peace. I don't give you the kind of peace that the world gives. So don't be troubled or cowardly"* s Vicarious death on the cross *(John 14:27 GWT).*

P69: *"Never take your own revenge ... leave room for the wrath of God." (Romans 12:19).*

P70: *"For ye are dead, and your life is hid with Christ in God" (Colossians 3:3).*

P70: *"Lord, how oft shall my brother sin against me, and I forgive him? till seven times? Jesus saith unto him, I say not unto* thee, Until seven times: but, Until seventy times seven. red and ninety times in one day! (Matthew 18:21-22).

P70: "For my yoke is easy and my burden is light" (Matthew 11: 30 NASB)

P71: "This is the covenant that I will make with them after those days, saith the Lord, I will put my laws into their hearts, and in their minds will I write them; And their sins and iniquities will I remember no more" God-fearing mind: (Hebrew 10:16-17).

P72: "I can do everything through Christ, who gives strength" (Philippians 4:13) NLT.

P72: "ask, and it will be given to you; seek, and you will find; knock, and it will be opened to you" (Matthew 7:7).

P72: "Strip off every weight that slows us down, especially the sin that so easily trips us up" (Hebrew 12:1 NLT).

P73: "And the tongue is a fire: the world of iniquity among our members is the tongue, which defileth the whole body, and setteth on fire the wheel of nature, and is set on fire by hell" (James 3:6 ASV).

Chapter Seven

P87: "Whether therefore ye eat, or drink or whatsoever ye do, do all to the glory of God" (1 Corinthians 10:31).

P88: "But Paul cried with a loud voice, saying, Do yourself no harm: for we are all here" (Acts 16:28 NASB).

P88: "Blessed are ye, when men shall revile you, and persecute you, and shall say all manner of evil against you falsely, for my sake" (Matthew 5:11).

P88: "But whosoever drinketh of the water that I shall give him shall never thirst; but the water that I shall give him shall be in him a well of water springing up into everlasting life" (John 4:14)

P89: "Submit yourselves therefore to God. Resist the devil, and he will flee from you" (James 4:7).

P89: "O give thanks unto the LORD, for he is good: for his mercy endureth forever" (Psalm 107).

P89: "Being found in fashion as a man, he humbled himself, and became obedient unto death, even the death of the cross. Wherefore God also hath highly exalted him, and given him a name which is above every name: That at the name of Jesus every knee should bow, of things in heaven, and things in earth, and things under the earth; And that every tongue should confess that Jesus Christ is Lord, to the glory of God the Father" (Philippians 2:8-11).

P90: "Subject to principalities and powers, to obey magistrates, to be ready to every good work, to speak evil of no man, to *be no brawlers; but gentle,* (showing) *all meekness unto all men" (Titus 3: 1-2).*

P90: *"And one cried unto another, and said, Holy, holy, holy, is the LORD of hosts: the whole earth is full of his glory" (Isaiah 6:3).*

P91: *"O LORD, our Lord, how majestic is your name in all the earth!" (Psalm 8:1-4 NIV).*

P91: *"Therefore if thou bring thy gift to the altar, and there rememberest that thy brother hath ought against thee; Leave there thy gift before the altar, and go thy way; first be reconciled to thy brother, and then come and offer thy gift" (Matthew 5:23-24).*

P92: *"go and tell (the villain) his fault between you and him alone" (Matthew 18:15).*

P92: "Thou shalt not hate thy brother in thine heart: thou shalt in any wise rebuke thy neighbour, and not suffer sin upon him" (Leviticus 19:17).

P93: *"if he listens to you, you have won your brother over" (Matthew 18:15b).*

P94: *"If (the villain) will not hear thee, then take with thee one or two more that in the mouth of two or three witnesses every word may be established" (Matthew 18:16)*

P95: "Stay wide-awake in prayer. Most of all, love each other as if your life depended on it. Love makes up for practically anything" (1 Peter 4:7-9 AB).

P95: "If he shall neglect to hear them, tell it to the church" *(Matthew 18:17).*

P95: "Do ye not know that the saints shall judge the world? And if the world shall be judged by you, are ye unworthy to judge the smallest matters?"saints will judge the world: (1 Corinthians 6:2)

P96: "And suddenly there was with the angel a multitude of the heavenly host praising God, and saying" (Luke 2:13).

P**Error! Bookmark not defined.**: "Give to the LORD the glory his name deserves. Bring an offering, and come to him. Worship the LORD in his holy splendor" **Error! Reference source not found.**

P97: "And, lo, the angel of the Lord came upon them" (Luke 2:9)

P97: "Thou preparest a table before me in the presence of mine enemies:" (Psalm 23:5).

P97: "There arose certain of the synagogue, which is called the synagogue of the Libertines, and Cyrenians, and Alexandrians, and of them of Cilicia and of Asia, disputing with Stephen" (Acts 6:9)

P97: "And suddenly there was a great earthquake, so that the foundations of the prison were shaken: and immediately all the doors were opened, and every one's bands were loosed" (Acts 16:26).

P98: "For we are the circumcision, which worship God in the spirit, and rejoice in Christ Jesus, and have no confidence in the flesh" (Philippians 3:3)

P98: "Declare his glory among the nations, and his marvelous deeds among all peoples"((1 Chronicles 16:24).

P98: "*For mine own sake, even for mine own sake, will I do it: for how should my name be polluted? and I will not give my glory unto another*" (Isaiah 48:11).

Conclusion

P100: *"And she shall bring forth a son, and thou shalt call his name JESUS"* (Matthew (1:21).

P100: *"I am not ashamed of the gospel of Christ: for it is the power of God unto salvation to every one that believeth; to the Jew first, and also to the Greek."* (Romans 1:16).

P100: *"All power is given to me both in heaven and in earth" (Matthew 28:18).*

P100: *"Does God indeed dwell on the earth? behold, the heaven and heaven of heavens cannot contain thee" (1 Kings 8:27).*

P100: *"God commendeth his love toward us, in that, while we were yet sinners, Christ died for us" (Romans 5:8).*

P100: *"For God so loved the world, that he gave his only begotten Son, that whosoever believeth in him should not perish, but have everlasting life" (John 3:16).*

P100: *"For the eyes of the LORD run to and fro throughout the whole earth, to shew himself strong in the behalf of them whose heart is perfect toward him. Herein thou hast done foolishly" (2 Chronicles 16:9).*

P101: *"if you forgive others for their transgressions, your heavenly Father will also forgive you. But if you do not forgive others, then your Father will not forgive your transgressions" (Matthew 6:14-15).*

P102: *"Jesus saith unto him, I say not unto thee, Until seven times: but, Until seventy times seven" (Matthew 18:22).*

P102: "And his lord was wroth, and delivered him to the tormentors" (Matthew 6:14).

ABOUT THE AUTHOR

Bishop /Dr. Uzziah Cooper Sr. is an inspirational speaker, dynamic educator and an effective Computer Engineer. Since 1984, he has been a regular contributing writer to The White Wing Messenger; a Church of God of Prophecy (COGOP) monthly publication.

Traveling extensively in the United States and other countries, he addresses critical issues effecting spiritual and social imbalance, with the central theme "beating the odds". Since 1983, Bishop Cooper has volunteered, unselfishly, most of his Ministerial Leadership Services to his church.

Presently, he serves the COGOP International office as Publications Editorial Task Force member, the COGOP Northeastern Region (NER), USA as Leadership Development Director and pastor of the Uniondale, NY Church; a ministerial role which he filled for a total of thirteen years both in Nassau Bahamas and the United States. Previously he served as District Presbyter, Hudson Valley & Capital District, NER, for seven years (2000 - 2007), Director, Center for Biblical Leadership (CBL), NER, for ten years, and CBL Instructor for the last twenty (20) years, both in Nassau Bahamas and the United States. From these areas of giftedness, he has developed the passion to effectively plant and grow local churches. His vocation, Computer Engineer – Virtualization, Networking, UNIX & Windows, supports his Pauline persuasion of "tent making"

Bishop / Dr. Cooper earned a Doctor of Ministry degree from Drew University, Madison NJ.; a Masters of Divinity degree from Church of God Theological Seminary; Cleveland Tennessee (1993), a Master's of Science degree from Florida Institute of Technology; Melbourne, Florida (1980), a Bachelor's of Science degree from Elmira College, Elmira NY (1980), and a member of The Association for Clinical Pastoral Education, Inc. (ACPE).

To contact

Bishop/Dr Uzziah B. Cooper Sr.:

Please email him:

ubcoopersr@abidingpromises.org

or

ubcoopersr@gmail.com

Do not forget to include your testimony

of

Blessings received through this book.

Your prayer requests are welcome.

Another Book by the Author:-

ISBN: 978-1-59684-391-2.

In spite of life's winding roads down unfavorable paths, every individual is assured victory through the promises of God. When mistakes of one kind or another propels disappointments, a glimpse through the eyes of faith can help to restore stability. A small reflection of the abundance promised through Christ can push the weak to say "I am strong".

Let's imagine the success and authority of the eagle for a moment. Because humankind has dominion over everything, every individual can soar above the eagle. Since Christ overcame the world, peace should not be forfeited any longer. No more should humankind dread the unknown! Abiding in the promises of God, assures good success.

Another Book by the Author:-

ISBN: 978-1-59684-516-9.

A *virtuous woman* is measured by her submission to her own husband and the values of her contributions to her children, society and to herself. Since she deserves accolades for the qualities which flourish within her life, *"her husband praises her" (Proverbs 31:28);* she is his Abigail. The husband's dominion to lead and the grace of his wife to submit form the key for a delightful marriage, but knowing their marital seasons is important.

Date your spouse and keep your marriage away from winter-dreariness. Praying together provides ever-green sprouting and spring-like blooming, but be aware of hay-fevers. Fall-like rust, yellow, brown or gold signifies a marriage's sunset. So Flirt with your spouse! Make "Emotional Bids" the building block of emotional connection and enjoy the harmonies of a pristine and dazzling summery skies of marriage!

Bibliography

Byrane, H. W. <u>Christian Education For The local Church:</u> An Evangelical & Functional approach. Zondervan.

Dorr, Luther M. <u>The Bivocational Pastor</u>, Broadman Press, Nashville, Tenn. 1988.

Douglas, J.D. & Tenney, Merrill; <u>The New International Dictionary of the Bible,</u> Regency Reference Library, 1987

Gerhard Lohfink <u>Jeusu and Community.</u> Fortress Press. Gangel, Kenneth O, <u>Building Leaders for Church Education</u>. Moody Press.

George, Bill <u>Ministry of Worship</u>, C of God Department of General Education, Cleveland, Pathway Press, 1985.

Johns, Cheryl B. <u>To Know God Truly - The Faith Community Model</u> in Theological Education Paper, *1994*.

Johnson, Susan <u>Christian Spiritual Formation.</u> Abingdon Press.

Land, Steve <u>Pentecostal Spirituality</u>, Sheffield Academic Press, Sheffield, 1993.

London, H.B. & Wisemann, Neil B. <u>Pastors at Risk</u>, Scripture Press Publishing   Inc., USA, 1993.

McMahan, Oliver <u>Becoming A Shepherd</u>, Cleveland, Pathway Press, 1994.

Reed, James E. & Prevost, Ronnie <u>A History of Christian Education</u>, Broadman & Holman Publishers, Nashville, Tenn. 1993.

Seymour, Jack L. and Miller, Donald E.. <u>Contemporary Applications to Christian Education</u>. Abingdon press.

Seymour & Wehrheim <u>Contemporary Approaches to Christian Education,</u> Nashville, Abingdon Press, 1992.

Stone, Howard W. <u>The Caring Pastor</u>, Harper and Row, Publishers, San Francisco, 1983.

Thompson, Frank Charles <u>The Thompson Chain-reference Bible</u>, NIV, KJV, B. B. Kirkbride Bible Co., Inc., 1987.

Thomas H. Groome <u>Christian Religious Education: Sharing our Story and Vision</u> (San Francisco: Harper and Row, 1980).

Walter Brueggemann <u>The Creative Word: Canon As A Model for Biblical Education</u>. Fortress Press.
Wilhoit, Jim <u>Christian Education and The Search For Meaning</u>. Baker Book House.

Zodhiates, Spiros <u>The Complete Word Study Dictionary, New Testament,</u> World Bible Publishers, Inc., Iowa Falls, Iowa, 1992.

SUMMARY

Unresolved conflicts bring our homeostasis into imbalance, for a couple or for a group. The spiritual dysfunctional persons within common groups are those who breathe-out conflict within the group. When they step out of bounds, and turn to *"Walking in the flesh" (Romans 8:2);* they give way to the lust of the eye, the lust of the flesh and to the pride of life.

Few will disagree that social ills feed the furious appetite of conflicts, with division and schism as their main ingredients. Their diet of divisions and schisms is heavily seasoned with hypocrisy, making a juicy serving of conflict sumptuous to the carnally minded person. Instead, all are reminded to gird up their pure minds for the fine cuisines of the spiritual food.

When each individual accept responsibility for their contributions to problem, instead of pointing out what others have done wrong to them, they will grow in character. Removing the log from our own eyes, will assure us spiritual vision for the putting on the whole armour to the honor and glory of God.

Endnotes

[1] Uzziah B. Cooper, Sr., *Abiding Promises,* Derek Press, Cleveland Tennessee, 2008 pp 131.

[2] http://www.carm.org/doctrine/holyspirit.htm, Reasoning from the Scriptures, (1985, pp. 406-407).

[3] Uzziah B. Cooper, Sr., *Abiding Promises,* Derek Press, Cleveland Tennessee, 2008 pp 170.

[4] Zalta, N Edward, *Stanford Encyclopedia of Philosophy*, Stanford University, Stanford, CA. 94305 8/2003.

[5] TBA

[6] People in Crisis, *Lee & Hoff,* Addison-Wesley Publishing Co. Inc. Redwood City, CA. 94065

[7] A.J. Tomlinson, *The Last Great Conflict*

[8] www.cyberhymnal.org/htm/m/i/mightyfo.htm

[9] Martin Luther, 1529, *A mighty fortress is our God, Words & Music:* (MIDI, score); translated from German to English by Frederi H. Hedge, 1853.

[10] Howard Haney, BEF.1927 (Attributed), *Keep on the Firing Line.*

[11] Matthew Henry's Concise Commentary on the Bible

[12] Longenecker, Dwight, *St Benedict and St. Therese: the little rule & the little way, (2002), 170.*

[13] Alexander, Donald L., *Christian Spirituality: five views of Sanctification -The Pentecostal View*, (Downes Grove, IL: Varsity Press, 1988), 148.

[14] Zaleski, Philip & Carol, *Prayer, A History,* (Boston, MA: Houghton Mifflin Company, 2005), 4

[15] Myron Rush, *Management: A Biblical Approach,*

[16] The New International Dictionary of the Bible, *p.392, add year.*

[17] The Message (MSG), *(2 Timothy 1:9).* by Eugene H. Peterson; Copyright © 1993, 1994, 1995, 1996, 2000, 2001, 2002

[18] The Message (MSG), *(2 Timothy 1:9).* by Eugene H. Peterson; Copyri ght © 1993, 1994, 1995, 1996, 2000, 2001, 2002

[19] http://uk.music.crossmap.com/view_lyrics.htm?id=629 Artist: Holland Davis, Copyright: 1997 Maranatha Music